AWESOME ELEMENTARY SCHOOL

PHYSICAL EDUCATION ACTIVITIES

BY

CLIFF CARNES

COPYRIGHT

© Cliff Carnes 1983
3949 Linus Way
Carmichael, California 95608

Illustrated By Sharon Pritchard

Odd/Even

Pick a number
from 1-10.

ACKNOWLEDGMENTS

My thanks and appreciation must first be given to my wonderful family whose help was essential to the writing of this book. My wife, Louise, gave her understanding and support during the long hours and involvement that this book required, in addition to assisting with organization and typing. My sons, Cliff and Jim, contributed to the development of many of the challenge activities that I have used in my programs throughout the years.

In addition to my family, I would like to give special thanks to Mark Sutherland, a teacher in the San Juan Unified School District. Mark is a professional juggler who has taught hundreds of children to juggle through his step-by-step, no fail approach, and many educators have adopted his method of teaching juggling. The Scarf Juggling section of this book was written by him. He and I collaborated on the Jump Rope, the Ultimate Challenge, and the Olympic Activities sections.

I next wish to thank Conrad Mizuno who is a Primary Physical Education Specialist and Title I All Purpose Resource Teacher for the San Juan Unified School District. Conrad developed many of the primary activities in this book with the purpose of increasing "student involvement time." His input regarding the way in which activities should be written and taught was valuable to this book.

I also want to recognize Kathy Geyer, K's Typing Service, for her superb editing and typing. Her cooperation, diligence, and expertise in the final preparation of this material is greatly appreciated.

And finally, my sincere appreciation must go to Sharon Pritchard, teacher in the Rio Linda Union School District. Sharon was the artist for this book whose attention to detail can be observed on every page. Her clever and precise illustrations have brought dimension and life to the written word. In addition to her teaching, she has authored three books: <u>Animal Cartooning</u>, <u>Fat Lettering</u>, and <u>Monsters</u>. Plus she has edited a new book, <u>A Guide for the Beginning Calligrapher</u>.

Flip A Coin

Rock, Paper, Scissors

Compromise the Distance

Play it Over

i

<u>Awesome Elementary School Physical Education Activities</u> is
an easy-to-use handbook which was developed with the classroom teacher in mind. Activities are offered which can put
more action into any existing program or help to fulfill
the objectives written for a new program.

Children should be actively involved during Physical Education. A goal, suggested by the author, for involvement
time would be 16 minutes of activity for every 20 minute
period of Physical Education. The games and activities in
this book are based on that premise. The skill building
and challenge activities are designed to encourage children
to develop to their greatest potential, whatever their
abilities may be.

A section of this book is devoted to collecting, creating,
developing, and using homemade equipment.

It is this author's hope that this book will provide teachers
with some new and different activities to add to their Physical Education program while, at the same time, increase the
fun and enjoyment for all involved.

Introductory Activities   Let's Go For It -

Cliff Carnes

Hot Hand

Start right hand to right
hand, close eyes, both spin
3 times in own personal space.
Stop and press right hands
together with eyes closed.

String Puzzle
Get yourself apart without
taking the yarn off the wrists.

TABLE OF CONTENTS

TABLE OF CONTENTS (Continued)

Vote On It

Longest Blade of Grass

Which Hand is the Coin In?

THE PERCEPTUAL MOTOR PROGRAM EXPERIENCE GOALS

Locomotor

1. Crawling
2. Creeping
3. Walking
4. Running
5. Hopping
6. Galloping
7. Leaping
8. Skipping
9. Rolling
10. Sliding
11. Stopping

Axial

1. Bending
2. Rising
3. Curling
4. Swinging
5. Swaying
6. Twisting
7. Falling
8. Tensing
9. Relaxing
10. Turning
11. Dodging
12. Pivoting
13. Stunts

Manipulative
(Objects)

1. Handling
2. Trapping
3. Catching
4. Carrying
5. Lifting
6. Throwing
7. Kicking
8. Striking
9. Pushing
10. Pulling
11. Bouncing
12. Rolling
13. Grasping
14. Releasing

Physical Education Strands (Ways to Go)

1. Perceptual Motor
2. Rhythms
3. Games
4. Movement Education
5. Dance
6. Centers
7. Command to Discovery
8. Skills Program
9. I CAN and CAN YOU Challenge Programs
10. New Games (Non-competitive)
11. Quiet Games
12. Fine Motor
13. Recreational Activities
14. Gymnastics
15. Multi-disciplinary
16. Physical Fitness
17. Team Sports
18. Holiday Celebrations
19. Competitive Activities
20. Task Cards

MOVEMENT EDUCATION CONCEPTS

1. To be successful with the program, the teacher must be in full control. Erratic behavior can and will destroy the program.
2. Spatial Awareness - where the student is in the room; how he maneuvers himself/herself around objects, other people; how close, how far away from the wall, etc.
3. Personal Space - the space that the student sees as his/her own to begin from and return to on cue. It may be a concrete object such as a mat, a tire, a hoop, etc.
4. General Space - the total useable space in the room. Everyone's space belongs to the general space.
5. Flow - the smooth uninterrupted continuity of one movement to another to create a pattern or a sequence of movements that may or may not be repeated.
6. Force - reflected by the tension of muscles as they project strong, moderate, or weak responses.
7. Time - to use or change the time of movement. Changing of time does not always change force.

THEME OF NEW PHYSICAL EDUCATION GOALS FOR CHILDREN

1. Self Image: Know body parts and how they work; have positive identification - know capabilities, relationship to self and others plus self expression.
2. Social Behavior: Know how to interact, produce, share, rebound from disappointment, accept success with humility, lead, and to follow. Have knowledge of elements or structure in order to know what is acceptable.
3. Motor Skills: "Greatest emphasis"
   A. Locomotor - Crawling, creeping, walking, running, hopping, jumping, galloping, sliding, skipping, leaping, rolling.
   B. Non-locomotor - Bending, stretching, rising, falling, swinging, swaying, pushing, pulling, tensing, relaxing, turning, twisting, dodging, pivoting, starting, stopping.
   C. Manipulative - Grasping, releasing, throwing, catching, kicking, striking.
   D. Perceptual - Kinesthetic, visual, auditory, tactile, eye hand, eye foot.
   E. Combined Movement - Without equipment, with large apparatus, small apparatus, creative games.
4. Physical Fitness: "To perform movements vigorously, with greater speed, for longer periods of time."
   The components are balance, endurance, strength, flexibility, agility, speed, and relaxation.
   The purpose is to develop heart, lungs, muscles, and joints through circuit training, movement education, task cards, specific exercise patterns, and interval training.
5. Interest in Recreation: To help students take initial steps toward the fulfillment of this goal, to become actively involved in worthwhile leisure time activities, knowing what leisure time activities are available.

A PHYSICAL EDUCATION PROGRAM

The Ideal Ingredients

1. A commitment on paper.
2. A staff commitment beyond the paper work.
3. A key person at the school who is emotionally involved in the program.
4. Tools and equipment.
5. Indoor space.
6. Adequate time set aside each day.
7. Instant lesson plans available.
8. In-service twice a year.
9. $2.00 per student set aside each year for new and replacement equipment from funds, PTA, etc., or a combination of sources.
10. A $500.00 starter for equipment from funds, PTA, or a combination of sources.
11. Parent help for perceptual motor or remedial program.
12. An extra person (teacher or aide) to work as a specialist within the program.

Directions

above	start
below	stop
in	in front of
around	over
away from	under
near	across
beside	forward
left	backward
right	each
stay	again
come	easy

Numerical Concepts

one	middle
two	none
count	some
once	all
many	any
few	group
first	class
last	several
next	begin

Body Parts

ankle	forehead	neck
arm	hair	nose
cheek	hand	seat
chest	head	skin
chin	heel	shoulder
ears	hip	thumb
elbow	knee	throat
eyes	leg	toes
finger	mouth	waist
foot	nail	wrist

Movement

walk	climb	melt	shake	crawl
hop	skip	relax	twist	catch
jump	gallop	swing	turn	throw
bounce	stand	straight-stiff	roll	watch
touch	balance	drop	reach	toss
leap	sit	lie	bend	stretch

Designs in Space

circle	curved	big - little
round	zig-zag	biggest
square	wide - narrow	smallest
line	long - short	open - close
straight	little - small	shut

MOVEMENT EDUCATION BASIC VERBAL CUES

Who Can	Show Me How	As You Listen to the Rhythm
In Your Personal Space	Can You Stand	Look Around the Room as You
Show a Change in Time	Who Can Fit	Using Different Parts
Change Your Direction	As You Walk	Can You Make Your Body
How Close	Facing Someone	Using Two Body Parts
Can You Do It Backward	Can You Move Like	How Low
Jump Over as	How Many Parts	While Keeping Time
Bounce and	While Resting	Can You Touch
Find a Partner	Looking to Your	Toss Above Your Head
While Moving	How Many Ways	Can You Skip
Roll the	Control Your	Travel in the General
Toss from Hand to Hand	How Would You	While It is Rolling
How Slow	Can You Fit	See If You Can
Can You Do It Fancy	What Other Ways	Without Touching Anyone
With Your Partner	While Walking	Can You Bounce Under
Who Can Twist		

Hula Hoops
Contests! **Games!** **Tricks!**
Relays! *Hoop Challenge* *30-30 Item* *30 players- 30 hoops*
Locomotor-Axial-Manipulative

Hula Hoops are made from 3/4" or 1/2" poly pipe normally used for sprinklers. The pipe can be purchased in 100' coils from any plumbing company. The diameter of the hoop is determined by the length. The cut lengths should be 3 times the diameter desired; 30" - 32" is a good diameter.

To weld ends together, (1) use doweling the size of the inside of the pipe, cut about 1" long, glue with Elmer's glue, and tape from the outside or (2) use 2-way repair stems for pvc pipe, purchased at the sprinkler shop. Use contact cement on the stems and tape on the outside. Also, use clear plastic tubing, the size of the inside of the pipe.

NOTE: If doweling or tubing is extra tight, put the end of the pvc pipe into boiling water for a few seconds until it expands.

NOTE: To repair kinks that arise from extended use, cut the kinks out and insert a plug.

Hula Hoop Challenges

Hoops Flat
Stand in your hoop and balance on one foot - other foot - other foot, eyes closed. Tall balance on one foot - low balance on one foot - reverse. Balance in your hoop on 3 body parts - try 3 other body parts. Let me see you balance on 5 body parts - now 5 with 3 inside hoop, 2 outside hoop. Can you jump up and down 5 times, each time jumping a little higher? Jump forward out of your hoop - jump backward into your hoop - jump backward out of your hoop - jump forward into your hoop - jump sideways out of your hoop - sideways into your hoop - sideways out of your hoop - sideways turn 1/2 turn. Long jump forward out of your hoop as far as you can - turn around and long jump into your hoop - "soft landing." Stand in your hoop - hop up and down 5 times on one foot - 5 times on the other foot. Hop all the way around the outside of your hoop - change feet and hop around the other way - hop around the hoop on one foot - land inside - outside - inside - other foot. Find your way to travel around the hoop.

Hoops Up
Hold your hoop above your head like this - drop it without letting it touch your body. Can you skip around in Angel Walk Position? Now pretend that you are driving straight up a mountain, twist and turn as much as you can - don't run into anyone. Spin your hoop like an eggbeater, let it spin low to the ground. Jump in and out without stopping it - use your hoop like a jump rope Hold your hoop straight up and down, jump in and out. Toss your hoop up, catch it before it touches the ground. Spin your hoop away from you with backspin - make it come back to you. Can you do it without moving your feet? Roll your hoop forward - run and catch it. Let me see you roll it forward and run around it as it rolls.

Hula Hoop Imagination

Spin your hoop around your arm, change arms without stopping the hoop. Can you spin your hoop around your neck? Let the hoop hang heavy around your neck - move around heavy like a big old work horse. Let me see the world's largest earring - can you do the earring hop? Change earring side and hopping side. Now let's be a walking mirror - don't use your hands to hold the hoop - how fast can you walk? Don't bump into anyone. Be a race car driver - use the hoop as your steering wheel - make lots of noise as you turn sharp corners - Go Fast!

1. <u>Game Switch</u>

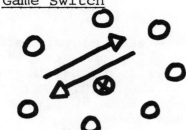

Hoops - Fast Record - MP Room
Break into 3 games.

The object of the game (switch) is to change
places with other players on the outer circle
without getting caught in center. Center player
can take an outside hoop anytime. The player
caught without an outside hoop, when the music
stops, takes a point and starts in center.

Motor skills reinforcement - skip, hop, gallop, run backward, etc.

2. <u>Musical Hoops</u>

Hoops - Fast Record - MP Room
Total Class - 30 Hoops - 31 Players

Players move around the room to various commands -
skip, hop, gallop, run backward, slide. When
music goes off, all players try to land in a hoop.
The "out" player takes a point and states next
motor skill challenge or type of movement.

A challenge can be posed for landing in a hoop when music goes off - be
a statue, land on 3 body parts, etc. Integrate Motor Skills.

3. <u>Flat Hoop Line Relays</u>

Different Types of Relays:

A. Leap over each hoop
B. Run around each hoop
C. Land in each hoop
D. Put each hoop over body

*   All of the above will turn into 15 more -
    change them around.

4. <u>Circle Standing Hoop
    Relays</u>

4 Games of 8 Players

Hoops are held vertical in front of body with
bottom of hoop touching the ground. On "Go,"
one designated player drops hoop, takes off,
crawls through all of the other hoops, picks up
own hoop. Next player takes off - when all
players have gone, relay is over.

5. <u>Hula Hoop Tag</u>

6 Hoops

Integrate the hoops into any tag game. Use the hoops as safety areas.
A player can stay in a hoop for 15 seconds before he/she has to move.

6. <u>Hoop Bumper Tag</u>

DIRECTIONS: Players are paired with both players
inside a hoop holding the hoop waist high. The
"It" hoop players are holding an object (either
player). The object is to identify them as "It"
players. All hoop players run around holding up
hoops. The "It" players attempt to bump another
hoop which is the same as tagging. The new "It"
players take the object and begin chasing other
sets of hoop players.
NOTE: 3 sets of "It" players with 30 players
make for an active game.

7. Poison Hoop

Fast Record - 4 Games - 8 Players - 2 Hoops
per Group

Four circles of players - each player holds hands
with other circle players. Hoops are placed over
arms of players. When music starts, players begin
to step through hoops to the left.
OBJECT: Not to get caught with hoop over body
when music goes off. Move fast.
VARIATION: Use one hoop - Poison Hoop Relays.
How many times can a team get the hoop around.

8. Hoop Patterns

Hopping, Jumping, etc. Many Patterns

9. Partners

Find a partner; exchange hoops by rolling them to
each other. Try it again. Give both hoops to
your partner. Let your partner make an obstacle
course - you travel through it - reverse.

10. Hoop Space Shuttle
Relays (Primary
Favorite)

Teams of four are lined up across the court. The
first player in each line is holding a hoop around
his/her waist. On "Go" - the first players take
off, run to the line and back. On returning, they
pick up the next player in the hoop and relay back
and forth, pick up the next . . . .
The first four players that cross the last line
in a hoop win the relay.

11. Balloon Four Hoop
Soccer

DIRECTIONS: Teams are divided equally (2); one
team should be wearing pinnies. Two players from
each team are designated to be Hoop Goalies for
their teams. The job of the Hoop Goalies is to
run around on the outside of the circle, while
holding hoops vertically, and encouraging team
members to kick the balloons through their hoops.
Team members on both teams have two functions -
to kick goals and to stop the other team from
kicking goals. Balloons are great! Balloons with
a super-ball inside are even greater - Total
Movement.

Hoop Tricks

Hula Hoopin' Craze
Hula hoop with the hoop
around your waist. 5-6-7-8-9-10
seconds!

Slip the Hoop
   Place your hoop flat on
the ground. Step into your
hoop. Get the hoop back
over your head and away
from you while using only
your feet.

Toss Spin and Catch A Hoop
Toss your hoop into the air. Spin your body all the way around. Catch the hoop.

Shoot the Hoop
Roll your hoop forward. Run through the hoop while it is moving. Can you make it back through?

Spin to Win - Backward
Spin your hoop like an egg-beater. Run around the hoop two or three times before it falls.

Circle Your Hoop

Roll your hoop forward. Circle your hoop 2 or 3 times before it stops. Make sure you have a lot of space.

Straddle the Hoop
Shoot the hoop away from you with backspin. As your hoop returns, straddle-jump and try to clear the hoop completely

Hula Hoop Jumpin'
1. Use your hoop like a jump rope.
2. Can you jump ten times backward without missing?

Arm Hoop Spinning

Spin your hoop around your right arm for one minute while you are walking around. Spin your hoop on your left arm for one minute while walking around.

Full Spin Land 'n Spring

Place your hoop flat on the ground. Run forward toward the hoop. Jump into the air, make a full spring with your body and land in the hoop. Spring out!

Ball Challenges

Ball Flat on Ground

Place the ball on the ground; stand behind your ball; jump over your ball. Let me see you jump back over your ball. Stand beside your ball. Can you jump sideways over your ball - jump back? Try it 3 times each way. Let's try hopping forward over your ball; turn around and hop back over; try it sideways. Hop all the way around your ball, now the other way. Spread out. Now let's try leaping. Leap over your ball, now back. We're ready to leap over 6 other people's balls and come back and stand in back of your ball. Jump over your ball, twist and end facing the other way - again.

Ball Up

Let's see how many ways we can hold the ball - up high, down low, in back, between your knees, between your elbows, back of your hands, right hand way high, low reverse. Hold the ball in your right hand, stand on right foot, lean forward; try your left foot, left hand. Now, right side again; only when you lean forward, close your eyes - reverse. Hold the ball in front of you, using just the finger tips of both hands. Can you spin the ball forward? Backward? Move the ball around your body - waist high, neck high, knee high. Move it between your legs, figure 8. Reverse. Reverse.

Dribbling

Can you dribble the ball waist high? Use finger tips only; other hand; alternate hands; both hands. How low can you dribble - other hand, both hands, alternate hands? How high can you dribble - control it, other hand, both hands, alternate hands? Now low - now high - low dribble and turn your body in a circle - other hand - other way. Change to a kneeling position while dribbling the ball; sit - kneel - stand up - kneel - sit. While dribbling the ball, get into a coffee grinder position; dribble all the way around. Try it with your other hand. Now we are ready to dribble the ball without looking at it. Walk around the room dribbling the ball without looking at it - finger tip dribbles, other hand, alternate hands. Move faster! Now, stay in one place, dribble in a circle without looking at the ball - again - other hand, other way. Place the ball in between your feet - jump up, toss the ball up and catch it with your hands. Let's experiment. How many other body parts can you dribble with? Great. Great... Now, let's hold the ball above your head and behind you. Drop it. Catch it behind your back. Bounce the ball hard; run underneath it; catch it facing the other way. Toss the ball up; jump up and catch it with your feet off of the ground. Toss the ball up - let it bounce - spin your body all the way around and catch the ball. Now take out the bounce. Now finger tip control. Can you volley the ball up with just your finger tips? Find a partner and volley a ball back and forth. Hold the ball way high; let it drop; catch it below your knees. Now do it again and clap 5 times before you catch it. Toss the ball up; step forward and catch it behind your back. Toss the ball up. How many times can you clap before you catch it? Dribble the ball; change hands as you dribble behind your back. Toss the ball up; let it hit your head and bounce behind you; spin your body around while clapping 5 times; catch it on the first bounce. Close your fist and strike the ball against the wall 5 straight times. Now walk while bouncing the ball from one hand to the other between strides - right hand under left leg - left hand under right leg, as you walk. Dribble the ball for 2 minutes without talking or missing. Count the bounces. Now, as you dribble, face me - as I flash a card, re-create the letter with your other hand while dribbling. Change hands.

Toss, Bounce, Spin 'n Catch

Toss the ball into the air, let it bounce.
Spin your body all the way around and
catch the ball on the first bounce.
Try two spins - catch it with one hand.

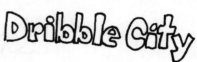

Continuous Dribbling

Dribble the ball for two minutes without
talking or stopping. Try dribbling with
your other hand.

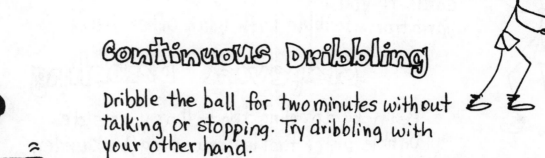

Ball Tricks

Position Dribbling

Stand and dribble, as you dribble move
to a sitting position, to your knees,
to your stomach, back to your knees
and come back to a standing position.

Dribble City

Dribble the ball around your body five
times without missing. Switch hands
as you dribble the ball.

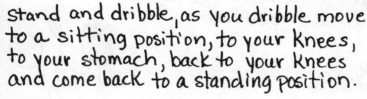

Shootin' Craze

Shoot five baskets within 20 seconds.
Retrieve your own ball and shoot like crazy!

Quick Hands

Hold the ball between your knees. One
hand in front, one hand around a leg.
Switch hands five times without missing.

Dribble 'n Re-Create

Dribble the ball continuously. As you dribble re-create ten letters or shapes with your free hand as your partner calls out or flashes cards to you.
Variation: Dribble with your other hand.

Grapevine Dribbling

Begin by dribbling the ball at your side. Dribble under first leg, second leg, back under, back under five times without missing. Use bounces in between if necessary.

Coffee Grinder Dribbling

Get into a coffee grinder position. Dribble the ball while moving around in a coffee grinder position.

Knee Action

Toss the ball into the air. Bounce it off of your knee once, then off of the ground once. Catch it and look good.
Variation: Bounce it off of your head.

Ultimate Challenge - Bean Bags

Toss your beanbag from behind your back. Right hand over left shoulder, left hand toss over right shoulder.
Place the beanbag in both hands behind your back, toss the beanbag overhead and catch it knee high in front of you.
Three consecutives catches completes the challenge.

Floor Ball - Curriculum Ball - Baffle Ball

Take a sheet of 2" thick foam and cut it into 2 x 2 x 8" strips. It takes 12 strips to make a ball. Stack them on top of each other evenly. Take a cord 36" long and tie it around the center of the strips. Put gloves on and pull it tight. Tie the cord even tighter than you think you can. Move the ends around a little and you have a ball. Put curriculum on the ends, numbers, vowels, blends, etc. You create the activity. These balls are also excellent floor balls for the MP room. They move slower during inside soccer type games.

Schermz

An old sweat sock with one or two old tennis balls shoved inside. Tie or rubberband just above the balls. A good object for catching, releasing, grasping, underhand tossing.

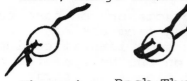

Schermz Activities
Keep Away   Toss for Distance   Target Toss

Wingers

Throwing, tracking, catching skill item (individual activity). Tennis ball and elastic. Elastic - 9' of 1/4" wide, old tennis ball, large needle, pliers.

Through   Back Through

Put elastic into needle. Push needle through center of ball, take pliers, pull needle all of the way through. Move needle over 1" and push needle back through ball. Tie elastic off on same side of ball. Make a loop at the other end to fit over wrist.

Loop   Tie Off

THROWING   ROTATE   TRANSFER   FOLLOW   TRACK AND
"CORRECT FORM"   THROUGH   CATCH

Feet Come
Even

Beach Balls

These are inexpensive purchase items. Beach balls are non-threatening as it does not hurt to get hit by one; and they can be used for Primary Dodge Ball, Soccer, Target Games, Volleyball lead up games, and a game such as hitting a rolling beachball with another ball.

Sportform Balls 8½"

These are semi-expensive. Purchase 6 balls from Physical Education Central Storage. They can be used for Dodgeball, Soccer, relays, and all types of games. This is the best buy in physical education as they are an all-purpose ball - kids can get hit in the back, face, stomach, and they will laugh! The approximate cost is $7.50, and they can be purchased as follows: Black Sportform Ball #H&S 37085 8½" diameter from Hammett & Sons, 1441 North Gum, Bldg. E, Anaheim, CA 92806; phone toll free 800-854-7189, California 714-632-8530.

Balloon Activities

Balloons are inexpensive; so attempt to purchase a better-than-average grade of balloon as they will last longer during activity sessions. Buy them by the gross.

Balloon Activities

1. Body Parts and Balloons

The teacher might make up some visual cards of body parts for students to see during activity. Keep the balloon up with your foot.

12" [FOOT]
14"

Use a good fast rhythmical record. Children will focus in on cards.

ankle	elbow	hand	mouth	shoulder
arm	eyes	head	nail	thumb
cheek	fingers	heel	neck	throat
chest	foot	hip	nose	toes
chin	forehead	knee	seat	waist
ears	hair	leg	skin	wrist

2. Pop or Be Popped
(Team Activity)

"Eye Foot"

Endurance

NOTE: Keep scissors on hand to cut string from ankles.
Pinnies, or some identification item, are placed on one half of the players. Each player ties a 36" string to a balloon and makes a loop around the ankle (loose loop). On "GO," one team tries to pop all the balloons on the other team. High Action! A great activity for getting rid of balloons for the day.

Balloon Challenges

Can you let the balloon fall and hit it up 2" from the ground? Can you spin? Sit down and try it. Partner tricks - players create their own tricks. Rainy day classroom balloon volleyball.

Fleece Ball

(Fleece Balls - SJUSD Stores - Price $1.32 Each)

Throwing Skills

Making Fleece Balls could be a classroom project; collect yarn from your students.

Basic Materials:
1. 2 skeins of yarn.
2. Cardboard circles (2 pieces, 5-8" in diameter)

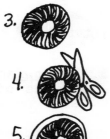

Directions:
1. Cut a round hole in center of cardboard 1-2".
2. Place cardboard together. Cut about 4 yards of yarn off the skein to start.
3. Wrap yarn around cardboard from center out. Cover the cardboard 2-3 times.
4. Tie the yarn off.
5. Take some sharp scissors and cut the yarn between the edges of the cardboard.
6. Take some cord or nylon string and wrap it between the cardboard. Tie it off; wrap and tie again.

PRESTO - A Ball. Trim the Ball.

Nylon Stocking Ball

Take an old nylon and some fibre fill (pillow stuffing); shove it into the nylon until it reaches the bottom. Twist the nylon stocking, put the fibre fill through, twist it again, put it through, twist ... until you have a little bit of stocking left. Take masking tape and close the opening or sew it. This is a non-threatening ball; make 16 for throwing and catching, and practice with your class.

Nylon Stocking Ball or Fleece Ball Challenges

Partner Tricks Individual Tricks

Can you -
1. Toss the ball into the air, clap 5 times before you catch it - both hands, left hand, right hand.
2. Toss the ball forward into the air, run 6-10 steps forward, catch it - both hands, right hand, left hand.
3. Hold the ball up high with both hands, release it, catch it - try catching it below knees, ankle height, clap __ times before you catch it.
4. Hold the ball up high with your right hand, release it, catch it again; same hand, catch it below knees - ankle height. This time, hold ball up, release it, reach across and catch it with other hand - below knees. Hold ball up with left hand and do all of the above.
5. Toss ball into air, sit down and catch it; toss ball up, stand up and catch it.
6. Toss ball up, spin all the way around and catch it.
7. Toss ball above head, step forward and catch it behind your back.
8. Put the ball between your feet, jump up and catch it with your hands.

9. Toss the ball up, jump up and catch it with both feet off the ground.
10. Find a partner. Make some fancy tosses and catches, using both balls at the same time.

NYLON STOCKING BALL OR FLEECE BALL ACTIVITIES

1. <u>Silent Dynamite</u> - Rainy Day Classroom
    All students sit on desk tops. Three yarn balls are tossed around room to players. If a student misses a good toss, he/she must sit down for 30 seconds or eliminate to 10 players. Start again.

2. <u>Throwing and Catching Skill Lesson:</u>

 Pull
Ball
Back

Rotate body

 Transfer
weight
forward

Follow
through

 Track ball
Catch with
hands

 Pull
ball
in

3. <u>Throwing and Catching Movement Activity</u> (Partners)
    Types of throws and tosses to make while moving.
    Put on cards - use fast record - keep moving

Jump Shot	Other Hand Shot Put	Side Arm Throw
Shot Put	Catch Over the Shoulder	Low Throw
Fancy Throws	High Catch	Roll It
Highest Point Throws	Other Hand Throws	Low Catches
Arc Tossing	Incorrect Throws	

4. <u>Bombardment</u> - Rainy Day (Large Group - MP Room)

Balls flying back and forth across center line. If a player gets hit with the ball, he/she goes behind the line and retrieves balls for the team. If a player attempts to catch a ball and drops it, that is the same as being hit.

Keep students out for
about 1 or 2 minutes,
then everyone in.

5. <u>Kung Fu!</u> (Large Group - MP Room) - Throwing
    Dump out all fluff balls. Students pick up one ball at a time, jump up into the air and throw the ball at other players while letting out a huge yell. While the music is on, how many players can you hit in the buns or toe.

6. <u>Clean Your Own Backyard</u> - Rainy Day (Large Group - MP Room)

Tossing (underhand). (Use fast record). Dump all 30 balls out in court. Turn on record. Students keep underhand tossing ball across center line. When the teacher shuts off the volume, players cannot toss another ball. Team with the fewest balls on side wins. Play several rounds.

NOTE: Try this with students sitting on floor.

7. <u>Star Wars Dodgeball</u>

Rebound Nets or substitute - yarn balls -
8 balls, 6 players in center. Self contained.
Game center players use nets to rebound balls
back. If a center player gets hit with the
ball, the outside player takes his/her place.
Tootie Rebound Nets

8. <u>Target Toss</u>

9. <u>Partner Tricks</u>

10. <u>Target Throws</u>

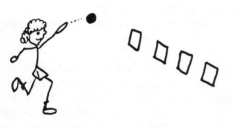

11. <u>Target Throws</u>

12. <u>Pickle</u>

"Chase the runner down."

13. <u>Total Class Challenge</u>

Toss the ball up, clap your hands three times

14. <u>Individual Tricks</u>

15. <u>Partner Tricks</u>

16. <u>Throwing Skills</u>

<u>Teacher Assists</u>

 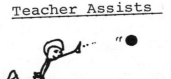

Ball Relays

1. Dribbling Relays

2. Basketball Pass

3. Pass n Duck

4. Stride Ball

5. Time Bomb

6. Over'n Over Relays
   (A total movement
   education relay)

Line up tight

7. Travel Relays

8. Return the Ball Relay
   Dribble, Pivot & Pass
   Relay

Ball Relays

Dribble right hand, left hand, both hands. Alternate hands - 3 spins while dribbling - sliding - other side and over the obstacles. Put ball between knees, jump down, run back. Foot dribbling. Create.

The lead player passes to all players in a line. When he/she passes to last player, he/she replaces first player and everyone moves over one place. Last player runs out to line and passes to number one player. When everyone is back in place, the relay is over.

Six lines of 5 each. The first player steps out 5 steps and faces the line. On "Go," he/she chest-passes the ball to second player; player catches ball, passes back, "ducks." First player passes to third, etc. When everyone has passed and ducked and ball is back to first player, relay is over. First player ducks.

Six lines of 5 each. Players stand in line with feet apart. On "Go," first players pass ball back between legs; all players follow suit until ball reaches last player. Last player runs to front and begins again. When everyone is back in place, the relay is over.

Six players stand in small circle and bounce passing ball randomly. When whistle blows or music goes off, the player with the ball stands still. Everyone runs behind him/her, and player passes ball overhead to end. The last player runs to front with ball; first team finished wins.

Six lines of five each facing backward. First player passes ball back, over head, then peels off and becomes the end of the line. The entire line moves backward. The whole team must cross the finish line. A Total Movement Education Relay.

Use 3 balls and 3 tires or hoops for each line. Players run to first tire, pick up ball, dribble it with best hand to next tire. Put ball in tire, pick up next ball, dribble with other hand to next tire. Put ball in tire. Pick up third ball and dribble around cone and back to first tire, while performing motor skill. Place ball in first tire and run to tag next player. (Short lines).

Teams of 4 are lined up at least 6 feet from other teams. Player #1 dribbles the ball to designated line 5-8 yards away. Player #1 crosses line, pivots and bounce passes ball to player #2 who must wait behind line until ball arrives. Player #2 dribbles across line, pivots and passes to #3. When all players are across line, the relay round is over. Start back the other way.

9. <u>Return to Start Relays</u>
   Passing, Catching,
   Pivoting, Dribbling

Players take position as shown in the diagram. On "Go," player #1 passes to #2, #2 pivots and passes to #3, #3 pivots and passes to #4, #4 dribbles around the cone and back to #1 position. While this is taking place, #1 moves to #2 and so on. This continues until everyone is back in place.

10. <u>Cooperative Ball Passing</u>

Teams of six. Divide the team into 2 rows of three. The 2 rows should be about 5 yards apart and facing each other. The first two players begin side stepping forth and do the same thing back. Set the number of passes that should occur while traveling in one direction. Set the type of passes also.

11. <u>Grape Fruit Relays</u>

Player places the 7" ball between knees and hops down the short distance in kangaroo fashion, deposits the ball in a waste basket, then retrieves it and runs back.

Task Cards For Continuous Relays   Grades 4-5-6
Each line leader should have a task card.

1. Dribble the ball down and back with your preferred hand.
2. Dribble the ball down and back with other hand.
3. Side step as you dribble the ball down and back with preferred hand.
4. Side step as you dribble the ball down and back with other hand.
5. Skip as you dribble the ball down and back with your preferred hand.
6. Skip as you dribble the ball down and back with other hand.
7. Gallop as you dribble the ball down and back with your preferred hand.
8. Gallop as you dribble the ball down and back with other hand.
9. Make 3 spins as you dribble down, 3 spins back with your preferred hand.
10. Make 3 spins as you dribble down, 3 spins back with other hand.

Each captain has this card. Teams relay continuously until each participant has completed 10 relays. "3-person teams are great."

1. <u>Combatives</u>

Players face off. Each player has a 7" ball and a football flag. Flag is tucked in back pocket of each player, same length of flag hanging out of each. On "Go," both players begin dribbling and, at the same time, attempting to pull each other's flag. Each time that a flag is pulled, one point is awarded to the winner. Continue.

2. <u>Dribbling Flag Tag</u>
   (Total Class Activity)

A non-elimination activity. The entire class begins with a 7" ball and a football flag. Flag is tucked in back pocket of each player, same length of flag hanging out of each. On "Go," each player attempts to pull anyone's flag. When a flag is pulled, the flag is brought to the teacher. The player without a flag runs to the teacher, receives the flag, slaps the wall, puts flag in pocket, and is back in the game (minimum penalty).

Trick: Toss the ball up. Sit down and catch it.

Trick: Toss the ball under your leg and catch it. UT = Switch hand and leg.

Trick: Toss ball up. Step forward and catch it behind your back.

Trick: Dribble the ball and skip, gallop, slide or hop.

Trick: Place the ball between your feet, jump up and catch it.

UT = Juggle two balls with one hand, ten catches.

Tennis Balls Only
UT = Ultimate Trick

UT = Juggle three balls, cascade pattern, ten catches.

Trick: Toss ball up. Spin body 360°. Sit down and catch it.

Trick: Create a trick, teach it to the class.

Trick: Time it! Toss two balls, one at a time, catch them on the first bounce. UT = Toss three balls, catch them on the first bounce.

Trick: Toss ball up, Spin 360° and catch the ball. #1 First bounce #2 No bounce. UT = Toss ball up, spin two 360° turns, catch the ball. #1 first bounce. #2 No bounce.

Trick: Toss the ball against a wall, spin 360°. #1 Catch the ball on the first bounce. #2 No bounce. UT = Spin two 360° turns, catch the ball, first bounce.

UT = Body juggle, Forearms, Knees, six taps.

Trick: Toss the ball up, let it bounce off the ground, then bounce off your knee, catch it #1 First bounce. #2 No bounces.

Trick: Toss ball from behind your back, over your shoulder and catch it. UT = Switch hands. Opposite shoulders.

Trick: Sit down, toss ball up. Stand up and catch it.

Trick:
Toss the ball from behind your back, catch it in the can. **UT** = switch hands!

Trick:
Toss the ball up, kneel down and catch it on the first bounce. **UT** = perform this trick, catch it before it bounces.

Trick:
Toss the ball up, spin 360°.
#1 Catch it on the first bounce.
#2 Catch it before it bounces.
UT = perform the trick, switch hands, spin the other way.

Trick:
Toss ball under your leg. Catch it in the can.
UT = Perform the trick, switch hands.

UT = Toss two balls up, one at a time, catch them on the first bounce

Trick:
Create a trick - Challenge the class!

Tennis Balls and Tennis Ball Cans
UT = **Ultimate Trick**

Trick:
Toss the ball against a wall, catch it on the first bounce.
UT = perform the trick, spin 360°, catch it on the first bounce.

Trick:
Toss the ball up, sit down, catch it on the first bounce.
UT = perform the trick, catch it before it bounces.

Trick:
Perform motor skill while balancing the ball on the upside down can.
Skip, gallop, leap, slide, hop...

Cooperative Trick
Create a fancy exchange of tennis balls and challenge the class. Innovate!

Trick:
Turn the can upside down, set the ball on the can. Thrust upward - the ball goes into the air. Flip the can over in your hand.
#1 Catch the ball in the can on the first bounce.
#2 Catch the ball in the can before it bounces.

Trick:
Toss the ball up, let it bounce, let it bounce off your knee -
#1 Catch it on the first bounce.
#2 Catch it before it bounces.

Arc the ball
UT = Toss the ball against a wall, catch it in the can before it bounces.

Trick: Hold ball in one hand and upside down, can in the other. Toss ball up, let it bounce, tap it up with bottom of can. #1 Flip can over, catch ball on first bounce. #2 Flip can over, catch ball before it bounces. **UT** = Perform trick, switch hands.

UT = Turn can upside down. Set the ball on the can. Thrust the can upward, let it go. The ball and the can will both be in the air. The can will flip over. Catch the can then catch the ball in the can on the first bounce. Catch the ball before it bounces.

Trick:
Tap the ball up ten times without missing.

Trick:
Keep the ball tapped up while walking forward, sideways, backward.

Trick:
#1 Low dribble twenty times.
#2 Dribble ten times in the same square.
#3 Write your initials while you dribble the ball.
#4 Dribble and turn in a circle.

Trick:
Tap the ball up ten times while flipping the paddle over each time.

Tennis Balls and Wooden Paddles
UT = Ultimate Trick

Trick:
Time it! Tap the ball up, let it hit the ground. Jump off the ground each time that you tap the ball.

Trick:
Balance the ball on your paddle while skipping, galloping, sliding, hopping...

Trick:
Locomote! keep the ball tapped up while skipping, galloping, sliding, hopping...

Cooperative trick:
Use one ball and create a fancy exchange and challenge the class.

Trick:
Tap the ball up - go to a kneeling position and back to a standing position.

UT = Tap the ball up. Go to a kneeling, then to sitting position and back to standing.

UT = Tap juggling. Keep two balls going by tapping, catching, tapping...

UT = Grapevine dribbling. Dribble the ball under each leg with taps in between. Try this from the other side with your other hand.

UT = Side paddle taps, six taps. Tap the ball up on the flat part of the paddle. When you feel ready, turn the paddle sideways and tap once on the edge of the paddle. Turn paddle flat and recover. Use as many recovery taps as needed.

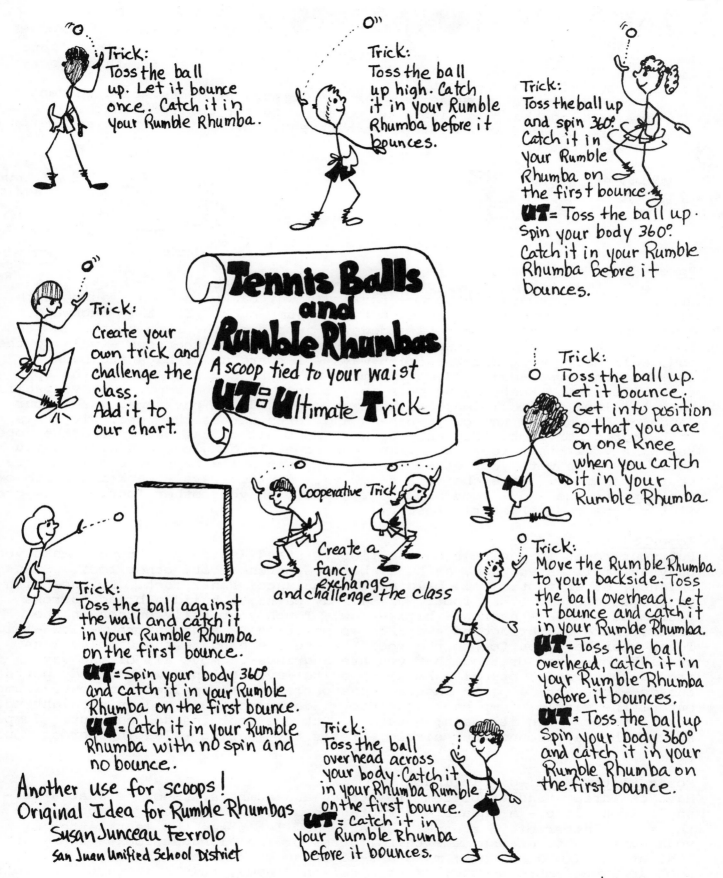

Trick: Toss the ball up. Let it bounce once. Catch it in your Rumble Rhumba.

Trick: Toss the ball up high. Catch it in your Rumble Rhumba before it bounces.

Trick: Toss the ball up and spin 360°. Catch it in your Rumble Rhumba on the first bounce.

UT = Toss the ball up. Spin your body 360°. Catch it in your Rumble Rhumba before it bounces.

Trick: Create your own trick and challenge the class. Add it to our chart.

Tennis Balls and Rumble Rhumbas
A scoop tied to your waist
UT = **Ultimate Trick**

Trick: Toss the ball up. Let it bounce. Get into position so that you are on one knee when you catch it in your Rumble Rhumba.

Cooperative Trick
Create a fancy exchange and challenge the class

Trick: Toss the ball against the wall and catch it in your Rumble Rhumba on the first bounce.

UT = Spin your body 360° and catch it in your Rumble Rhumba on the first bounce.

UT = Catch it in your Rumble Rhumba with no spin and no bounce.

Trick: Toss the ball overhead across your body. Catch it in your Rhumba Rumble on the first bounce.

UT = Catch it in your Rumble Rhumba before it bounces.

Trick: Move the Rumble Rhumba to your backside. Toss the ball overhead. Let it bounce and catch it in your Rumble Rhumba.

UT = Toss the ball overhead, catch it in your Rumble Rhumba before it bounces.

UT = Toss the ball up. Spin your body 360° and catch it in your Rumble Rhumba on the first bounce.

Another use for scoops!
Original Idea for Rumble Rhumbas
Susan Junceau Ferrolo
San Juan Unified School District

Note: Try all tricks with the Rumble Rhumba tied to the other side of your body.

Jump Ropes

Jump ropes can be cut from donated rope or purchased in quantities. Rope should be flixible, cotton, 3/8" to 1/2" in diameter. Stiff, thin, inexpensive rope will not make it.

1. Cut rope (all purpose lengths) 8' or have students stand in center, feet together, pulling rope to arm pits for desired length.
2. Tape or wrap ends of rope with thread, then tape to make sure ends will not unravel.

Jump Rope Challenges

Ropes Flat - In a Line

Jump both feet around rope, straddle rope, jump to end, jump back, turn around, jump backward and back - forward down, backward back - jump to the end landing on opposite sides each time - jump back. Try this backward, down, and back. Face the rope sideways; jump over the rope to the end and back, facing the rope sideways. Stand on the end of the rope - walk to the end, walk back, walk backward both ways - forward down, backward back. Straddle the rope again. Jump up, make a ½ turn and land facing the opposite direction. Keep trying this as you move down the rope. Get yourself into the lame dog position, one hand on each side of the rope. Keep your hands on the ground as you jump back and forth across the rope. Try this with your other foot. Hop on your best foot all of the way around the rope. Hop with your other foot, hop down your rope, landing on each side as you hop. Try this with your other foot. Try this while hopping backward; try your other foot. Face the rope sideways. Hop sideways - back and forth over the rope to the end - come back. Try this with your other foot. Criss-cross walk to the end. Faster! Faster!!

Ropes Flat - In a Circle

Put your ropes in a circle on the floor. Stand inside your rope. Make your body as small as you can, as huge, balance on one foot; other foot. Swan balance; other foot. Tall balance, low balance; other foot. Balance with your eyes closed; other foot. Use 4 body parts to build a bridge across your pond - huge - narrow - high - low. Touch your belly button on the floor. Make the bridge backward (crab position) - huge, narrow - low - high. Touch your belly button to the roof. Place one hand in the circle, legs straight out, and pretend that you are a grinder. Move all of the way around the circle; opposite hand; opposite way. Balance with 2 body parts inside - one out; 4 parts inside - one out; 3 parts inside - one out. Jump out of the circle; jump backward into, sideways out; in. Jump straight up. Make a ¼ turn. Do it again; ½ turns. Put one foot inside, one out. Jump all of the way around your circle. Let's try leaping - leaping across your pond.

Ropes Flat - Multi-disciplinary

Have children stand at bottom of letters and numbers. Show me what a triangle looks like - a square - a rectangle. Let me see how you would make the first letter of your name. Great! Now let's see the last letter of your name. Show me what the third letter of the alphabet looks like - 5th - 7th, etc. Find a partner; make a 2-digit number; make a consonant blend. Hook up with 2 more people; print a person's name, only 4 letters. By yourself, add 5 + 4; make the answer with your rope. Draw the Eskimo's house.

Can you make a 5 sided figure? What do you call it? Let me see a vowel sound - all at once, yell out your vowel sound. Print a 2 letter word, the first with your rope, the second with your body (all caps).

JUMP ROPE CHALLENGES (Continued)

Pretend Series
Invent the world's largest earring - longest beard in the world - coolest moustache - braided hair - world's largest shoestring - karate belt. Invent a telephone - cowboy rope - hospital patient - world's largest bow tie.

Ropes Up
Hold both ends of the rope in your right hand. Turn the rope rapidly, making the loop touch the ground each time. Turn it backward; other hand; forward; back; turn it each side. Change hands each time. Turn circles in front of body while touching ground - clockwise, counter clockwise - each hand. Don't stop - above head - helicopters - other hand. Can you jump your own shot? Take the rope in your best hand, turn the rope at your side; jump in rhythm as the rope hits the ground near your feet. Try it with the other hand. Turn the rope with your right hand; hop on your left foot in rhythm. Find a partner; one holds both ropes - turn both ropes at the same time, jumping as the ropes touch the floor.

Other Jump Rope Activities

1. __Ropes__   2. __Motor Skill Tool__   3. __Rat Tails__ Eye/Foot   4. __Leap the Brook__

Run in between each rope - increase challenge - ropes closer together and farther apart

Musical ropes

Tuck rope in back of pants or pocket. Step on opponent's rope. Make the rope drop to the floor

2 ropes flat - increase distance

Exercises

1. Hold over head (rope doubled) stretching both ways.
2. Half the rope behind neck; pull - hold 5 - release.
3. Half the rope behind waist; pull - hold 5 - release.
4. Stand on rope; pull it up - hold 5 - release.
5. One foot on rope, stick leg out straight; bend leg up high; leg to side; leg in back; other leg.
6. Fold rope - 1/4 of rope - pull under chin - hold 5 - release.
7. Wring the dishrag - twist rope.
8. Hold rope straight, arms out, step through rope - back.
9. Tie 6 knots in _____ seconds.
10. Sit down; double rope and hold out in front on a line - feet over, feet under, etc.

Double bounce forward jump

Single bounce forward jump

Single bounce Right foot forward jump.

Single bounce left foot forward jump

Double bounce Right foot forward jump.

Double bounce forward jump. Left foot forward jump

Double Bounce

Right foot Backward jump

Double bounce Left foot Backward jump

Double bounce Backward jump

Single bounce Backward jump

Single bounce Right foot Backward jump

Single bounce Left foot Backward jump

Two Additional Tricks

Movin' On Step over the rope 20 times as you jog down the blacktop.

Jog In Place Step over the rope 20 times as you jog in place.

Suggested Routines
  Put the six forward jumps together in a continuous routine by having students move from one trick to the other without stopping. Use four bounces for each trick.
  Use the same method to enrich the backward jump.

Jump Rope Clubs- Red, White and Blue Clubs

  The first 12 tricks could be considered Red Club tricks.
Pass all tricks in the Red Club prior to moving to the White Club.

Side Swing Note:
Do not cross hands when swinging the rope to the sides of the body.

Double Side Swings
Swing the rope on one side of the body, then swing it on the other. Open the rope and jump through. Repeat.

Single Side Swing
Swing the rope on one side of the body. Open the rope and jump through. Swing the rope on the other side, then jump through. Repeat

Skier

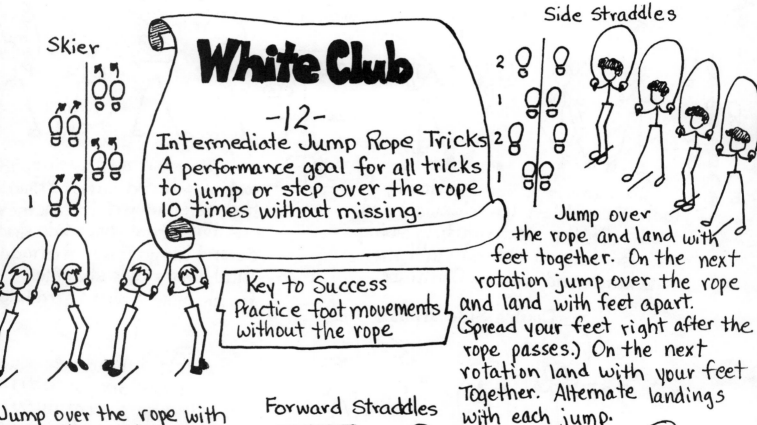

White Club

-12-

Intermediate Jump Rope Tricks
A performance goal for all tricks to jump or step over the rope 10 times without missing.

Key to Success
Practice foot movements without the rope

Jump over the rope with feet together while moving horizontally to one side of a line about 4". On the next rotation move across the line and land about 4" on the other side. Keep feet together and turn toes in a little. Stay in rhythmn.

Side Straddles

Jump over the rope and land with feet together. On the next rotation jump over the rope and land with feet apart. (Spread your feet right after the rope passes.) On the next rotation land with your feet together. Alternate landings with each jump.

Forward Straddles

Jump over the rope and land with feet spread apart vertically 8-10". Land with the right foot in front. On the next turn of the rope land with left foot in front. Continue jumping while changing forward foot each time.

Forward Swing Kicks

Step over the rope onto left foot. Extend right leg forward. On the next rotation swing right leg down and extend leg forward. Alternate each rotation.

Side Swing Kicks

Step over the rope onto left foot. Extend right leg sideward. On the next rotation swing right leg down and extend left leg sideward. Alternate on each rotation.

Side Steps

Step over the rope onto right foot. Extend left leg sideward and touch. On the next rotation swing left leg in and extend right leg sideward and touch. Continue...

◄12"►

Double Straddles

Putting it all together. To combine side and forward straddle. Feet never return to together position. First jump = Side straddle. Second jump = Forward Straddle. Third jump = Side straddle. Fourth jump = Forward straddle.

Double Side Steps

Step over the rope onto right foot. Extend left leg sideward 5" and touch. On the next rotation step over the rope on the same right foot again and extend left leg about 12" out and touch (a Double Step to the Left). On the next turn of the rope swing left leg in and move right leg 5" out and touch. Continue...

Suggested Routine:

Put any six jump trick together in a continuous routine. Students move from one trick to the other without stopping. Use four bounces for each trick. Students select tricks.

X to Straddle

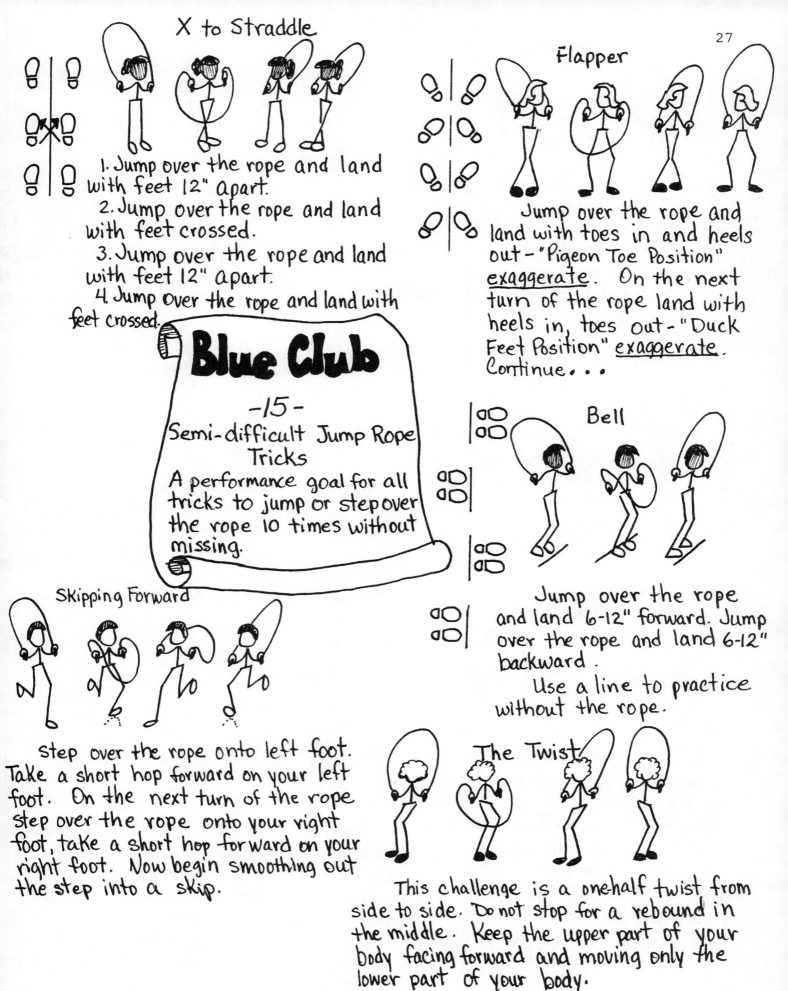

1. Jump over the rope and land with feet 12" apart.
2. Jump over the rope and land with feet crossed.
3. Jump over the rope and land with feet 12" apart.
4. Jump over the rope and land with feet crossed.

Blue Club

-15-

Semi-difficult Jump Rope Tricks

A performance goal for all tricks to jump or step over the rope 10 times without missing.

Flapper

Jump over the rope and land with toes in and heels out - "Pigeon Toe Position" underline exaggerate. On the next turn of the rope land with heels in, toes out - "Duck Feet Position" exaggerate. Continue...

Bell

Jump over the rope and land 6-12" forward. Jump over the rope and land 6-12" backward.

Use a line to practice without the rope.

Skipping Forward

Step over the rope onto left foot. Take a short hop forward on your left foot. On the next turn of the rope step over the rope onto your right foot, take a short hop forward on your right foot. Now begin smoothing out the step into a skip.

The Twist

This challenge is a onehalf twist from side to side. Do not stop for a rebound in the middle. Keep the upper part of your body facing forward and moving only the lower part of your body.

Heel Touch

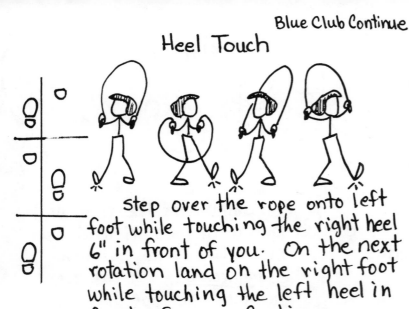

Step over the rope onto left foot while touching the right heel 6" in front of you. On the next rotation land on the right foot while touching the left heel in front of you. Continue...

Toe Touch

Step over the rope onto left foot while touching the right toe next to the left heel. On the next rotation land on the right foot and touch the left toe next to the right heel. Continue...

Hot Peppers

Go for it! Turn the rope and jump as fast as you can - 20 jumps in 10 seconds!

Heel to Heel Cross and Go!

Step over the rope onto left foot, touch right heel forward 6". On the next turn of the rope land on left foot again, cross right foot in front of left foot, touch right heel on outside of left foot. On the next rope rotation land on right foot and touch left heel forward 6". Continue...

X to Swing Kick

1. Jump over rope, land in X position, right over left.
2. Step over rope, land on left foot, extend right leg sideward.
3. Jump over the rope, land in X position, left over right.
4. Step over the rope, land on right foot, extend left leg sideward.

Toe to Toe Cross and Go!

Step over the rope onto left foot, touch right toe next to heel on inside of left foot. On the next rotation land on left foot again, cross right foot behind left foot, touch toe next to heel on outside of left foot. On the next rope rotation land on right foot, touch left toe inside of right heel. Continue...

Crossies   Blue Club Continue

Double Under   29

1. Cross arms as the rope swings down. Tuck and jump.
2. Uncross arms as the rope and arms come overhead. Jump.
3. Cross arms as the rope swings down. Tuck and jump.
4. Repeat #2.   Continue...

A faster turn of the rope, a higher bounce and a bend at the waist is necessary to prepare for a Double Under. As the rope approaches a downward swing, whip the wrists quickly. Two passes under the feet on one bounce = Double Under.

Knee Fling

On the first bounce bring left knee up while pointing toe toward floor. Skip the rope with the right foot. On the next bounce kick left leg straight out in front of you as high as you can. Switch over to bouncing on left leg. Continue...

Foot to Knee Fling

Step over rope onto left foot, touch left knee with right foot. On next turn of the rope rebound on left foot again, fling right leg sideward. On next turn of the rope land on right foot, left foot up, touch right knee. Continue...

Partners Chain

Partner Tricks

Partners jump while holding on to one end of partners rope.
Note: Add jumpers to your chain.

Partners Jump/Turn

Two in a rope. Partner faces away, turns 180° to face partner. One turn for each jump.

Partners Join In

1.
2.
3.
4.

Added: Hot Peppers!
25 jumps in 10 seconds.

Run through the turning rope. Easy directions.

Run through the turning rope. Hard Directions

Run to center. Jump 8 times. Run out.

Run to center. Jump 8 times. Two turns in each direction. Run out.

Long Turning Ropes

Performance Goal for all tricks is to jump 8 times without missing.

Run to center. Jump 8 times. Jump in a new direction every time.

Long turning ropes should be cut about 18' long. Use good 3/8" or 1/2" or 5/8" rope. Inexpensive stiff rope will not make it.

Run to center. Jump with right foot 8 times. Run out.

Run to center. Jump with left foot 8 times. Run out.

Run to center and touch the ground after each jump, 8 times. Run out.

Run to center. Bounce a ball 8 times. Run out.

Start in center. Jump with a short rope 8 times. Run out.

Run in center. Jump 8 times with a short rope. Run out.

Partners run through a long turning rope. Try 3 people. How many can you include? Easy direction.

Partners run through a long turning rope. Try 3 people. How many can you include? Hard direction.

Run to center. Partners jump 8 times. Run out.

Run to center. Partners jump 8 times, two turns in each direction. Run out.

Run to center. Partners jump 8 times in each direction, they turn and run out.

Run to center. Partners jump 8 times, right foot only. Run out.

Run to center. Partners jump 8 times, left foot only. Run out.

Run to center. Partners touch the ground after each jump. Run out.

Run to center. Partners bounce pass a ball after each jump. Run out.

Run to center. Partners exchange places while jumping. Run out.

Run to center. Partners exchange places using a Hoola Hoop. Run out.

Run to center. Partners jump with a short rope.

Long Turning Rope Continued

Start in center with Hula Hoop. Jump 8 times. Run out.

Run in center with a Hula Hoop. Jump 8 times. Run out.

Double Dutch. Two ropes turning inward. Begin with basic jump rope tricks.

Egg Beater. Two ropes turned by four people. Ropes turned across. One rope turned clockwise, the other rope turned counter-clockwise. Begin with basic turning rope tricks.

Jump the Shot

Combatives

Limbo

Leap Over the Brook

Jump Over

Pass Each Other

Walk the Rope

Going Through School K-12

Run through = K
Jump once, run out = 1st
Jump twice, run out = 2nd
Jump three times, run out = 3rd
Jump four times, run out = 4th
Jump five times, run out = 5th
etc.

First grade run in, jump once, run out. Second grade run in, jump twice, run out. • • •

Going Through School Activity by Audrey Cox
San Juan Unified School District

Bean Bags

Super Primary - Regular - Rectangle - Triangle - Circle

Find durable remnants and cut them 1/2" larger than Bean Bag size.
Stitch on a sewing machine from inside; go over seams at least 3
times. Turn right side out; fill and stitch last side. Fillers:
sand, beans, rice, popcorn, feed from feed store, bottle caps, etc.

Bean Bag Challenges

Bean Bags on Ground - Locomotor Tool
Stand in front of bean bag - stand beside bean bag - stand in back of
bean bag. Jump over bean bag - jump backward over bean bag. Can you
hop all the way around it? Now, with your other foot, let me see you
hop over sideways - now, back over. Now, let me see you build a bridge;
touch your belly button on the bean bag. Show me 3 great push ups.
Let's create some other bridges. Can you make one more? While we are
on the ground, let's get into coffee grinder position with your extended hand on the bean bag. Travel all the way around your bean bag
in coffee grinder position. Try using your other hand; go the other
way. Stand a few feet away from your bean bag - run toward it - jump
up and click your heels right over the top. Try it again. Now, let's
skip around the room to the music. When the music goes off, land on
your bean bag and be a great statue. Now, let's go again, only this
time let's move backward; don't bump into anyone . . . .

Bean Bags Up
Participants can be sitting, kneeling, standing, depending on the
challenge. Put the bean bag between your feet. Can you jump up and
toss the bean bag into your hands? Try it again; that's fun! Toss
the bean bag into the air, clap once, touch your shoulders once, catch
it .... Toss it up again, touch your knees, clap, touch opposite
shoulder, catch it .... Toss it up, clap 3 times, catch it with other
hand - start with your other hand. Hold the bean bag in one hand, toss
it back and forth to the other hand without moving your head - how wide
can you go? Can you catch it 10 times? Toss the bean bag up, run
under it and catch it - you should be facing the other way. Practice
time. Hold the bean bag as high as you can with both hands, release
it, catch it again. Do this again, only clap before you catch it.
This time, catch it after it has fallen below your knees. Release
it, touch your shoulders, catch it. Let's think of some other ways
that we could do this. Now, let's hold the bean bag in one hand as
high as you can - release it, catch it. Now, try it again, only catch
it below your knees. Now, let's work your other hand - same thing.
Now, we're ready for reaching across. Hold the bean bag up with your
left hand - release it - reach across and catch it with your other hand.
Practice. Now, other hand - below the knees catch. This time, toss
your bean bag straight up - sit down and catch it. Now, toss it up
from sitting position - stand up and catch it. Sit down. Place the
bean bag between your feet, rock back and touch the bean bag on the
floor behind your head. Now, lie down and place the bean bag on the
ground behind your head, rock back and pick the bean bag up with your
feet. Stand up, toss the bean bag up. Walk under it and catch it
behind your back. Toss bean bag up - spin your body all the way around
and catch it.

Bean Bag Freeze Tag

Bean Bag Freeze Tag - Line Tag

Bean Bag Egg Toss

Bean Bag Toss n Duck Relays

Bean Bag Relays

Bean Bag Patterns

Each player is given a bean bag to place on some body part - head, shoulders, arms, etc. - as directed by the teacher. Three people have an object such as fluffball, deck ring, whiffle ball, etc. These players are taggers; they also have on bean bags. They chase players and try to hand them or touch them with the object. If they do tag them, the newly tagged players are "it" players and are after everyone. Rule: If a chased player drops the bean bag, he/she is frozen until another player comes by and bends down, picks up the bean bag, and places it on him/her. If an "it" player drops the bean bag, he/she can put it back on the body part and continue.

Same game as Bean Bag Freeze Tag, only <u>all</u> players must stay on the line of a basketball court. Players can place bean bags on shoulders, elbows, head, etc. Use an object to hand off to a tagged player.

Players begin lined up down the court standing across from each other (12' distance). One player tosses the bean bag to partner, and partner tosses it back. If no one drops it during the tosses, both players step back one step and begin again, each time stepping back in successful exchanges. The team that can expand the farthest distance with perfect catches, wins. If one player misses, players return to start.
ADD: Right hand only - Left hand only

Toss the bean bag to each player and back. Each line player ducks after tossing bean bag back. The first team finished, wins.

Wear the bean bag on different body parts.

Back to back, around the back, two beanbags. Faster!

Bean Bag Tricks

Under, over. Get it going!

Toss the bean bag to the same person each time. Add 2,3,4, more bean bags as you become successful. Groups of 8-10.

Fancy Catch

#1 Toss your beanbag above your head. Catch it on top of your head.

#2 Toss your beanbag above your head. Catch it with your hands behind your back.

Jump, Toss 'n Catch a Bean Bag

Place your beanbag between your feet. Jump up and toss the beanbag into your hands. Try to catch the beanbag three straight times.

Tilt 'n Catch a Beanbag

Place your beanbag on top of your head. Tilt your head forward and catch the beanbag between your knees.

Toss, Spin 'n Catch a Beanbag

Toss your beanbag into the air. Spin your body all the way around and catch the beanbag.

Bean Bags   Passing

1. Make up a fancy routine. Add a third beanbag.

Reach Under and Catch It

Toss the beanbag straight up so it will fall straight down close to one side of you. Use the hand on that side of your body to toss it up. Bend down and reach between your legs with the other hand and catch the bean bag just outside of your leg. Do this on both sides of your body.

High Toss, Spin and Catch
Bean Bag

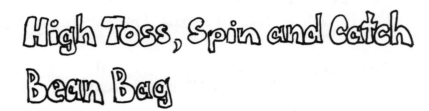

Toss your beanbag up, spin 360° and catch the beanbag behind your back. You may have to spin 360°+ some in order to catch the beanbag.

Bean Bag Return

Lay down with your legs straight. Place the beanbag behind your head. Sit up, rock back and pick up the beanbag with your feet and return to a sitting position.

Toss 'n Change Positions

#1 Toss the beanbag ten feet into the air. Sit down and catch it.

#2 Sit down, toss the beanbag as high as you can. Stand up and catch it.

Release It 'n Catch It

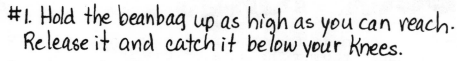

#1. Hold the beanbag up as high as you can reach. Release it and catch it below your knees.

#2. Hold the beanbag up with your other hand. Release it and catch it below your knees.

#3. Hold your beanbag up. Release it and catch it below your knees with your opposite hand.

High Toss 'n Catch

Toss the beanbag up as high as the room ceiling. Catch it with both hands. Catch it with one hand. Catch it with your other hand.

Jump Up - Time It - Catch It !

Toss the beanbag high into the air. Jump completely off the ground and catch it at the highest point. Time it so that both feet are off the ground when you catch the beanbag.

Swing 'n Catch

Place the beanbag on your best foot. Swing your foot upward and catch the beanbag with your opposite hand.
Place the beanbag on your other foot and do the same.

Deck Rings

Deck rings can be made from a garden hose that is ready to be discarded and clear plastic tubing the size of the inside of the garden hose.

1. Cut hose into 18" lengths.
2. Purchase 6' of clear plastic tubing at a hardware store. Take a piece of hose with you to the store to insure that you will get a tight fit.
3. Cut tubing into 2½" pieces.
4. Insert tube into end, pull ends together, glue and tape circle tightly and round. <u>Tape will fill gap.</u>
5. You have it - Durable Deck Rings!

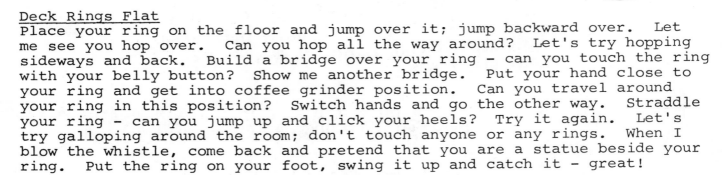

Deck Ring Challenges

Deck Rings Flat
Place your ring on the floor and jump over it; jump backward over. Let me see you hop over. Can you hop all the way around? Let's try hopping sideways and back. Build a bridge over your ring - can you touch the ring with your belly button? Show me another bridge. Put your hand close to your ring and get into coffee grinder position. Can you travel around your ring in this position? Switch hands and go the other way. Straddle your ring - can you jump up and click your heels? Try it again. Let's try galloping around the room; don't touch anyone or any rings. When I blow the whistle, come back and pretend that you are a statue beside your ring. Put the ring on your foot, swing it up and catch it - great!

Deck Rings Up
Toss the ring into the air; clap 3 - 4 - 5 times before you catch it. Toss it again and clap -- -- --. Catch it with right hand; try catching it with your other hand. Now, toss right hand - catch left hand. Don't forget claps. Now, left - catch right. Hold the ring with your right hand and toss to left hand without moving your head. How wide can you go? Let me see 5, 6, 7, 8, 9 perfect catches. Toss the ring up; run under it; catch it, facing the other way. Now, toss it higher; spin your body all the way around and catch it. Let's work on that for a while. Hold the ring up as high as you can - release it - catch it. Do that again, only clap before you catch it. This time, release it - clap - catch it below your knees. Show me how you can hold it up with one hand; release it and catch it again; now, catch it below knees. Try this with your other hand and catch it. Remember that we need to develop both sides. Try your other side. Let's practice the below-the-knee catch. Now, we are ready for spearing - release it with one hand, reach across and run your hand through the center, catch it on your wrist - other side - now, below the knees catches. Toss the ring up, sit down and catch it. While sitting, toss ring up, stand up and catch it. Now, let's toss the ring up in such a way that you can catch it over your wrist - use either hand for tossing. Now, toss it up and catch it over both hands and use wrists. Sit down, straighten legs and place the deck ring between your feet. Now, rock backward and touch the ring to the floor behind your head; now, rock back. Stand up, toss the ring up - walk under and catch it behind your back. Toss the ring up, spin your body around twice and catch it. Toss ring up - sit up, sit down, stand up and catch it.

Trick: Release, Reach and Spear It.

Hold your deck ring up in one hand, release it. Reach across and spear it with other hand. Other hand-spear below Knees.

Trick: Toss the ring up, sit down and catch it. Toss the ring up, stand up and catch it.

Trick: Toss ring into air, spin 360° and catch it.

UT = Toss ring into air, spin 360°, sit down and catch it.

UT = Try to toss ring with your other hand.

UT = Toss ring from behind back. Toss your ring from behind your back. Right hand over left shoulder, left hand over right shoulder, two consecutive catches.

Deck Rings Only
UT = Ultimate Trick

Trick: Rock Back Lay down flat on the floor. Place the ring about 6" from your head. Rock back and touch the ring with your feet.

Trick: Place the ring between your feet, jump up and catch it.

Trick: Toss ring into air, let it fall below your knee-line. Reach out and catch it with your opposite hand. Reverse.

UT = Juggle two deck rings with one hand. Six catches.

UT = Toss deck ring flat into air, spin body 360° and catch it on your foot.

UT = Try spinning in the other direction.

Trick: Place a deck ring in each hand. Toss one across body into air, then toss the other. Catch them in opposite hands.

UT = Five perfect exchanges. Toss – Toss – Catch – Catch.
1   2   3   4

UT = Reach Under. Toss ring into air, reach right hand under left leg and catch it. Reverse.

Trick: Toss ring into air. Step forward and catch the ring behind your back.

Trick: Create a trick.

Trick: Toss the ring under opposite leg and catch it with your other hand.

UT = Catch ring with the same hand used to toss the ring.

UT = Toss ring into the air. Spin your body around twice. Reach out and catch the ring.

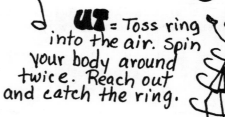

Rhythm Sticks

Sticks Flat on Ground - Locomotor

Stand in back of your sticks; jump over them; back over. Stand beside sticks; jump over them; back over. Jump over 5 times, each time a little higher. Jump end to end. Straddle stick; jump up and face the other way. Now, let's try some hopping. Hop back and forth 4 times over your sticks. Try it with other foot. Hop around 3 other sticks; come back to your sticks and touch your nose on them. Try moving your stick by blowing on it. Balance with 3 body parts touching your stick - 3 other body parts. Build a bridge over your stick - try another bridge. This time, balance your stick on your stomach and become a moving bridge. Now, stand behind your sticks. Balance on one foot and lean forward over your sticks as far as you can; close your eyes. Let me see you do this with your other foot. Now, get down in coffee grinder position and grind some coffee as you turn your sticks with your hand. Now, let's put the stick between your feet - jump up and catch it in your hands.

Sticks Up

Put the stick between your knees and walk around - faster - walk backward - sideways. Take the stick and pass it around your ankles - fast - knees, waist, other way, chest, neck. Pass the stick in a figure 8 position around your legs - reverse. Hold the stick vertically in front of your eyes; pass it back and forth without moving your head. How wide can you go? Take the stick and spin it on the floor - other hand. Balance the stick on your head, shoulder, elbow, knee, foot; swing your foot upward and catch your stick. Balance your stick on some body part and walk around. Hold the stick vertically in front of you; drop it; let it bounce and catch it - other hand. Drop with one hand and catch it with the other. Flip your stick over and catch it on the other end. Flip the stick over so that you catch the same end that was tossed. Toss it with one hand and catch it with the other hand. Now, hold the stick with one hand and roll it forward with your fingers. Do this with your other hand. Hold stick vertically and climb it, climb back down - other hand.

Hold the stick vertically at the very bottom, release it and grasp it again at the top so that none of the stick is showing at the top. Let me see you do this with your other hand.

Hold the stick up high in front of you with both hands, release it, catch it again. This time, catch below knees, release it; clap and catch it. Release it, touch shoulders, catch it. Now, hold the stick up high with one hand, release it, reach across and catch it. This time, catch it below the knees - reverse.

Two Sticks

Hold one stick like a nail and hammer the other stick through your hand - other hand - other way. Try this with your eyes shut. Hold sticks on ends; hammer them together until they pass through hands. Now, do this without looking. Flip both sticks at the same time; catch them on the other end. Flip them and catch them on the same end.

Create a Trick.

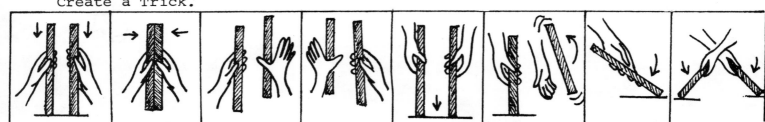

Patterns

One student taps a pattern, other follows.

Mirroring

Mirror your partner.

Spin 360° and catch your stick.

Rhythm stick passing

Balance sticks on two different parts of the body and walk around.

Rhythm stick hockey with a tennis ball.

Rhythm Stick Activities

Can you do this?

Challenge your partner with tricks-flipping and catching sticks, cross your arms.

Balance the sticks start with one stick, create tricks.

Rhythm stick hockey. Put a styrofoam cup target in the middle.

Catch the stick.

tick jousting on a rope.

Make partner change grip.

Stick Bull Dog Pull.

Ring Toss

Three Rings Up

Hurdle

Step Through

Wands

Wands can be cut from 1/2 to 5/8" doweling or from pvc plastic pipe. Cut wands 24-32" long, depending on the level. Pvc pipe wands are durable enough to use as wands, physical fitness activities, and soft enough to use as hurdles.

WAND CHALLENGE ACTIVITIES

Wands Flat on Ground - Locomotor Challenge
Stand beside your wand, balance on one foot, other foot, close your eyes, reverse feet. Build a bridge across your wand; touch your belly button on your wand; touch your nose. Show me a new bridge - one more. This time, build a bridge with 3 body parts on one side and 4 body parts on the other. Now, get down close to your wand and huff and puff to move your wand by blowing it with all of that stored up air in your body. Now, balance again in swan positions - lean forward as far as you can and close your eyes. Let's try that with your other foot. This time, stand beside your wand and jump sideways over it. If you jumped sideways over your wand 5 times continuously, which side would you be on after your last jump? Let's try it. Now, let's do that with a goal in mind. Jump over your wand 5 times; each time, going a little higher. Great! Now, stand facing your wand and jump forward over it; look behind you and jump backward over it. This time, pretend that you are about to set the new school record for the standing long jump. Get your toes up close to the wand, crouch, pull arms back and thrust your body forward like this - go! This time, use your arms more to pull yourself forward - go! Good effort! Now, let's try some wand hopping. Hop all of the way around your wand. Face your wand, hop over, hop backward over. Now, hop all of the way around on your other foot, over, backward. Hop the length of your wand, while landing on one side; then, the other. Now, try doing that while hopping backward. Hop around the room until you have hopped over 5 other wands one time. Next, straddle your wand. Jump up and rotate your body so that you land facing the other way while straddling it. Do 4 rotation straddles in a row. Now, let's play musical wands - one wand short. When I turn on the music, I want you to skip around the room in all of the general space. When the music goes off, select the closest wand, build a low bridge, and make your belly button touch. Next time, make a statute over the wand. Cover up wand so that none of it is showing - galloping, walking backward, etc. Now, let's get 8 players together and put wands end to end in a line. Each time, the leader selects a new way to travel down the string of wands. Change to a new leader each time that you start down the wands. Now, put them in a circle and follow the leader. This time, all 8 of you must create a movement game with your wands. You have 3 minutes. Go! Show time.

Wands Up - Manipulative
Balance your horizontal wand on the palm of your hand, back of your hand, two fingers, one finger; other hand. Now, on the back of your first hand, go to your knees, sit, lie down, sit, kneel, stand; other hand. Try balancing your horizontal wand on your elbow, head, shoulder, knee, other

knee.   Place the wand on your foot, flip the wand up, catch it with your other hand - right foot - left hand - reverse.   Balance your vertical wand on the palm of your hand and walk around the room.   Now, balance it on two fingers, one finger, walk.   Now, balance your vertical wand on the palm of your hand.   Do not take a step and hold it for 10, 20, 30 seconds. Now, do that on two fingers, one finger; other hand.   Hold your wand vertically in front of you, release it, let it bounce and catch it; other hand.   Drop it with one hand, catch it with the other; reverse.   Now, hold it up as high as you can and let it bounce, release it, catch it; same hand; other hand, etc.   Hold the wand vertically in front of you, pass it back from hand to hand without moving your head.   How wide can you get your hands?   Pass it around your neck, your shoulders, wrist, knees, figure 8.   Hold your wand in front of you, vertically, again. Hold it at the bottom, release it, and grasp it at the very top so that none of the wand is showing; time it perfectly.   Now, let's see you do that with your other hand.   Stand your wand on end with one end touching the ground like this ....   Release it, spin your body all the way around and catch it before it hits the floor; other hand; other way.   Start from a deep knee bend position, release, spin and catch; other hand; other way. Stand your wand on end again, release it and swing your leg over it. Catch it before it hits the ground.   Try it outside of your leg, inside of leg; other leg; release one hand and catch with other, etc.   Hold the wand horizontally (both hands) in front of you.   Now, step over it, step back over.   Now, hold the wand over your head; move it over your head, down your back, and then, step over it.   Now, hold it horizontally out in front of you; sit down and stand up.   Try doing that and cross your legs as you sit; then, stand up.   Now, you are ready to go to your knees, sitting on your back, on your stomach, on your back, sitting, kneeling, and standing.

Catch your partners stick before it falls

Two down the stick

Wand Bull Dog Pull

Two hand pull across

Change grips

To elevate wand for jumping, hurdling, leaping or going under practice

Wand Imagination

Scarf Juggling
by Mark Sutherland

1. Holding the Scarf
DIRECTIONS: Take the scarf and hold it, as seen in picture #1. Grab the middle of the scarf (x in picture) with your thumb, index, and middle finger. This is called the Jellyfish Position. Hold the scarf with palm down at waist level.

2. Basic Throw and Catch
DIRECTIONS: While holding the scarf, lift your arm as high as you can reach. Just before you reach the highest point, gently flick your wrist and release the scarf into the air.

Let the scarf float down and catch it at waist level, palm down, and with your thumb, index, and middle finger - Jellyfish Position. Practice with right and left hand.

3. One Scarf Throw and Catch
DIRECTIONS: While holding the scarf in one hand, bring your arm across your body and release it at the highest point. (Remember to gently flick your wrist.) Let the scarf float down and catch it in Jellyfish Position with the opposite hand.

Example: Right Hand Throws - Left Hand Catches (Scarf caught on the left side of the body.)

4. Two Scarf Throw and Catch
DIRECTIONS: Hold the scarves in both right and left hands at waist level - Jellyfish Position. Lift your right arm across your body and release the scarf on the left side of your body. Lift your arm across your body and release the scarf on your right side. (Your arms have made an x pattern.) Catch the scarves at waist level. First, catch with left hand; then, right hand - Jellyfish Position.

Verbal Cues: Right Hand - Left Hand - Catch - Catch - Repeat.

5. Holding Three Scarves
DIRECTIONS: Make a Jellyfish with the <u>first</u> scarf. Place it in your hand and wrap your little finger and ring finger around the scarf. Do not stick the scarf in between fingers. Grab the <u>second</u> scarf, in Jellyfish Position, with thumb, index, and middle finger of the same hand. Grab the <u>third</u> scarf - Jellyfish Position - with your other hand. Place it between thumb and middle finger.

6. Three Scarves - One Throw
DIRECTIONS: Hold the scarves in Jellyfish Position. Lift and release the scarf that is held by the thumb, index, and middle finger in the hand that has two scarves. Lift and release it on the opposite side. Let it drop to the ground

7.   Three Scarves - Two Throws

DIRECTIONS: Hold the scarves in Jellyfish Position. Lift and release the #1 scarf (front scarf). Then, lift the scarf from the other hand, #2, and release it on the other side of the body. "Remember to reach under the first throw when reaching across." Let both scarves fall to the ground. The scarves should land on the opposite sides of the body. See Illustration.

Verbal Cues: "Right and Left" or "One and Two" or "Black and Red."

8.   Three Scarves - Three Throws

DIRECTIONS: Hold the scarves in Jellyfish Position. Lift and release the front scarf from the hand which has 2 scarves in it, #1. Then, lift the scarf from the opposite hand, #2, and release it on the opposite side. Lift and release the remaining scarf on the same side as the first scarf, #3. Let all of the scarves fall to the ground.

Verbal Cues: "Right and Left" or "One and Two" . . .

9.   Three Scarves - Three Throws - Three Catches

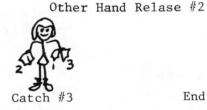

Start   Lift and Release #1   Other Hand Relase #2

Catch #1   Catch #2   Catch #3   End

Verbal Cues: Right - Left - Right or One - Two - Three or Color of Scarves or Lift - Lift - Catch - Lift - Catch - Catch.

10.   Three Scarves, More than Three Throws

DIRECTIONS: Hold the scarves in Jellyfish Position. Lift and release the first scarf in the hand that has 2 scarves, #1. Then lift the scarf from the other hand, #2, and release it on the opposite side. Grab the first scarf, #3, with the other hand. Grab falling scarf #2 and lift and release scarf #1, again with other hand. Grab scarf #3 and release scarf #2 with other hand. Continue ... alternate throws with each hand. Remember Verbal Cues!!!

Verbal Cues: Right - Left - Right - Left - Right - Left - One, Two, Three, Four, Five, Six.

Juggling

Basic Tricks and Patterns

by Mark Sutherland

These tricks can be done with scarves and balls. They can also be done with slight alternations with clubs, rings, and other objects. Once you've learned all these patterns and tricks, put them in a sequence, and you will have a juggling routine.

*   *   *   *   *   *   *   *   *   *   *   *   *

TWO IN ONE HAND

1) Begin with 2 in preferred hand

2) Raise arm - release one scarf

3) Release second scarf when first scarf reaches peak of height

1. Side by side

2. In a circle

Tips for scarves - Keep scarves same height. Keep scarves in same space as if they are on a string.

FULL 360° Turn

Juggle Cascade Toss #1 - high up the middle

Catch #2

Pivot 360° Turn

Toss #2

Return to the Cascade pattern

Hints: Pivot on one foot with arms held close to body. After turn is completed, be sure to toss scarf up before catching the high tossed center scarf.

TENNIS LOB

R. Toss #1

L. Toss #2
L. Catch #1

R. Toss #3
in half
circle
R. Catch #2

L. Toss #1
L. Catch #3

R. Toss #2
R. Catch #1

L. Toss #3 in
half circle
L. Catch #2

R. Toss #1
R. Catch #3
Repeat pattern

3   1 & 2   3
Pattern

Note: #3 always goes in a half circle R to L then L to R
over the criss-cross pattern (figure 8) of #1 & #2.

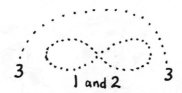

SINGLE COLUMNS

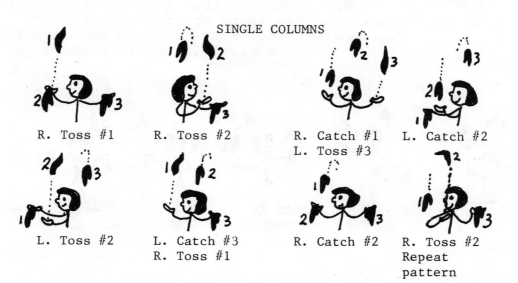

R. Toss #1

R. Toss #2

R. Catch #1
L. Toss #3

L. Catch #2

L. Toss #2

L. Catch #3
R. Toss #1

R. Catch #2

R. Toss #2
Repeat
pattern

Middle scarf will alternately be thrown by left and right hand.
Right side scarf will always be thrown by right hand.
Left side scarf will always be thrown by left hand.

COLUMNS

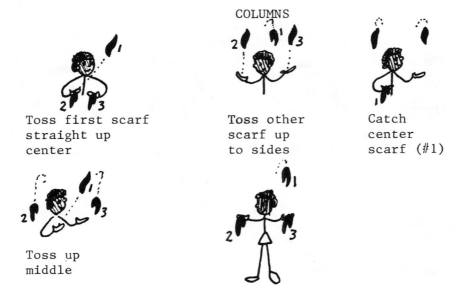

Toss first scarf
straight up
center

Toss other
scarf up
to sides

Catch
center
scarf (#1)

Toss up
middle

Hint: Scarves stay in stay position and order.

Pattern

Note: First scarf thrown always stays in
the middle. Scarves in right and
left hands always go straight up
at sides and return to the same hand.

*   *   *   *   *   *   *   *   *   *   *   *

SHOWERS

Pattern   Toss #1   Toss #2   Quick   Catch #1
                                             toss #3   Toss up #3

Quick Toss   Catch #2
#1   Toss up #1

Practice pattern with one scarf.
Try two scarves. With three
scarves, toss two scarves before
the third scarf enters the pattern. Scarves go in one direction
in a circle. Repeat pattern.

*   *   *   *   *   *   *   *   *   *   *   *

UNDER THE LEG

STEP 1   STEP 2   STEP 3   STEP 4   STEP 5

Juggle cascade, then:

Step 1:   Toss scarf from left hand higher than normal.
Step 2:   Simultaneously raise right leg and release scarf
          under it.
Step 3:   Lower leg and catch scarf with right hand.
Step 4:   Catch scarf with left hand; toss scarf with
          right hand.
Step 5:   Resume Cascade pattern

MAUI

STEP 1   STEP 2   STEP 3   STEP 4   STEP 5

Start by juggling cascade -
Step 1 - Toss one scarf up middle
Step 2 - When middle scarf descends, toss the scarves
         from right and left hands simultaneously
         across to opposite hands
Step 3 - Catch the middle scarf
Step 4 - Toss middle scarf up, then catch outer scarves
Step 5 - Resume cascade pattern

 *   *   *   *   *   *   *   *   *   *   *   *

HALF REVERSE CASCADE

One scarf   Two scarves   Over-Under - Over-Under
                                         Three Scarves

Establish pattern with one scarf. Dominant hand always
throws scarf in high half circle. Opposite hand always
throws scarf with a small straight up toss about chest
high. Using three scarves, the throws go: over - ½
circle; under - small toss (chest high); over, under.
Repeat continuously.

 *   *   *   *   *   *   *   *   *   *   *   *

FULL REVERSE CASCADE

Toss second scarf   Each hand alternately   Repeat
over the first   throws over scarf in
                             the air

Establish pattern with one scarf (figure 8 pattern).
Practice with two scarves. With three scarves, alternately throw scarf from right and left hands in small
half circles. Hint: Toss should land in your other
hand just past chest of center midline of body.

Figure  8

PATTERN

Partner Cascade

Stand side by side. Inside hands behind back, outside hands hold scarves. Throw scarves alternately to partner with outside hands. Try doing different patterns.

Dueling Jugglers

stand back-to-back

Take 3 paces while juggling.

Turn and cascade as fast as possible. Winner is the person that juggles longest without missing.

One Scarf Exchange

With partner, juggle cascade.

Toss one scarf high and exchange positions.

Partner Juggling

Take-a-Away

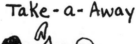

stand face-to-face with partner, one person juggling.

Partner reaches in alternately grabbing scarves from the cascade pattern.

Partner now juggles. It's your turn to take scarves back.

Continue cascade using falling scarf in pattern.

Totem Pole

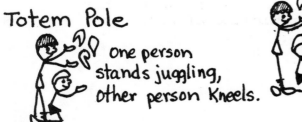

one person stands juggling, other person kneels.

standing person alternately releases scarves to kneeling partner who begins juggling.

kneeling person juggles and tosses alternate scarves up to partner.

Juggling Tips
(Mark Sutherland)

1. Use different colored scarves - it is easier to identify which
    scarf is to be thrown next.

2. Use the terms "lift" and "release." Throwing the scarf is in-
    accurate and results in the scarf going in the undesired direction.

3. Emphasize height - reaching as high as possible is essential
    for one to have enough time to keep the scarves going in the
    pattern.

4. Demonstrate - visual and repeated demonstration gives others
    an idea of what to do.

5. Use verbal cues - needed to help most people in teaching jug-
    gling. Use cues such as numbers - 1, 2, 3; colors - red, brown,
    green; hands - right, left, right.

6. In some cases, physically grabbing the arms of the learner and
    manipulating his arms in the rhythmic pattern helps break re-
    peated pattern errors.

7. Once one can do the cascade pattern for 10 throws, one has
    become an official juggler. Awards or certificates could be
    given to reinforce this.

8. "Not giving up" must be continually emphasized for learners
    to overcome frustration. Relate examples and personal ex-
    periences of similar motor activities where not giving up
    leads to success.

9. Start a juggling club. Once one learns the cascade pattern,
    many other tricks can be made up, taught, and learned. Every-
    one can help teach their peers of others.

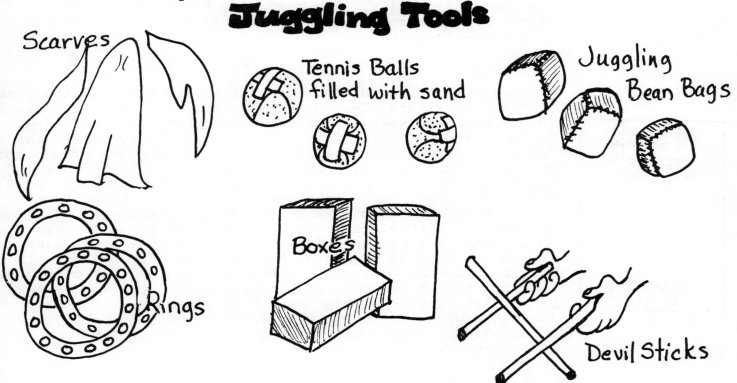

Juggling Tools

Scarves

Tennis Balls
filled with sand

Juggling
Bean Bags

Rings

Boxes

Devil Sticks

Chasing Fleeing Games

Use of Flags

Flags on Players save a lot of hassles!

One line games   Two line games

Boundary Games

Primary Favorites

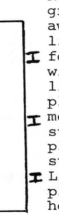

RED LIGHT-GREEN LIGHT

Red Light-Green Light can be played on the blacktop or
grass. The head player stands on a line about 20 yards
away from the line players. The line players stand on a
line facing the head player. The object of the game is
for the line players to walk or shoot past the head player
without him/her detecting or seeing them move. The first
line player to get past the head player becomes the head
player for the next round. If a line player is detected
moving, he/she can be sent back to the initial line or 5
steps back, depending on the rules. The game is best
played for success with 3 groups of 10. The head player
starts the game by turning his/her back and yelling "Green
Light." Line players advance. At any time, the head
players can yell "Red Light" and turn around. When the
head player turns around, he/she begins detecting players
who are still moving. The head player must yell "Red
Light" before turning around. If he/she doesn't, players
stay where they are.

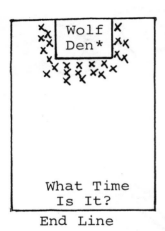

What Time
Is It?

End Line

MIDNIGHT

Midnight is a game that has one initial tagger, and the rest
of the players are flee type participants. A court, a little
larger than the size of a basketball court, is designated.
The one tagger is the "Wolf." The fleeing players are the
"Sheep." The wolf is designated to be in the key of one end
of the court or a small pen. The sheep skip out into the
meadow and around the pen. The sheep begin asking the wolf
what time it is. If he/she replies, "8:00," "10:00," or
any time other than midnight, the sheep continue skipping
around. If a sheep asks for the time, and the wolf says
"Midnight," all of the sheep run back across the end line and
try to avoid being tagged or having their flag pulled. If
they are tagged, they go to the wolf's den and sit down.
When the game gets down to 10 or so, a new game is started.
Do not let players sit for over 2 or 3 minutes. Football
flags are great for stopping arguments about being tagged.
ALTERNATIVE: Tagged players can also become wolves and
tag sheep.

TOUCHDOWN

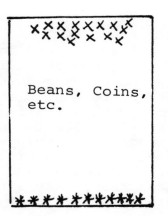

Beans, Coins, etc.

Players are designated to each end of the field - one team has on pinnies; both teams have flags in their back pockets. Teams huddle and decide who holds the beans. Each player closes his fists as if he were holding the beans. They yell "here we come." The object is for the person holding the beans to make it across the opposing team's goal line without getting his flag pulled. The teams should end at the oppo-site ends of the field. Each team gets 2 turns, then the other team gets 2 turns. One point is given for a touchdown. A player who has a bean in hand and does not get his flag pulled, scores a touchdown. When the team huddles, people that have already had the objects, close fists so that every-one gets a chance to carry the ball. The defensive team attempts to pull everyone's flag in order to catch the ball carriers.

SACK THE QUARTERBACK

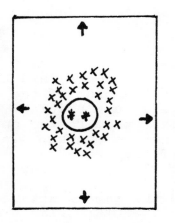

Two players are selected to be sackers. The rest of the players are quarterbacks. The job of the sackers is to en-courage quarterbacks to come as close to the circle as pos-sible, then, at a split-second, they yell, "Sack." The quar-terbacks take off and attempt to get across the line before their flag is pulled. If their flag is pulled before they cross the line, they become sackers and help out the other sackers. NOTE: Variation to increase intensity and skill - have each quarterback come into the court bouncing, or tos-sing up, a 7" ball, or some object. When the signal to run is yelled, the quarterbacks retrieve their balls and run.

ROCK, PAPER, SCISSORS

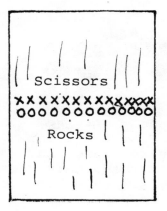

Scissors

Rocks

Players on both teams come to the line. Each team has a plan. After the usual Rock, Paper, Scissors ritual, the team comes down with one category. Rock smashes scissors, scissors cut paper, paper covers rock. If one team has rocks and the other has scissors, rocks chase scissors. All players tagged become players on the other team or go out and perform a task. Play until one team disappears. Both teams do the ritual at the same time! Teams come to line with two plans in case teams come up with the same sign the first time. Use flags when possible.

CROWS AND CRANES

Safe Line

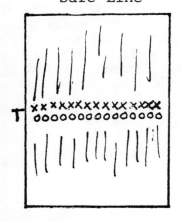

Crows and Cranes is a two equal-team line chasing, fleeing game. The teams line up about 3' apart facing off. One team is called the Crows, the other, the Cranes. There is a boundary about 10 yards behind each team. On a signal, the teacher calls out either Crows or Cranes, both teams are anticipating. If the teacher calls out Cranes, all Cranes retreat as fast as possible back across their own 10 yard safety line, while the Crows give chase and attempt to tag them in some way. Each Crane player tagged becomes a Crow. This can go until one team gets down to 5 or whatever is relevant for your grade level. Begin again. Football flags are great to use to avoid the arguments of "I tagged you - no you didn't." When the flag is pulled from the back pocket, that's IT. NOTE: Alternative - Leave tagged players out until one team gets down to 5. Hopefully this will happen in 2 or 3 minutes. Out players can also jump rope or jog around the perimeter, etc. NOTE: This game can be changed to many names, depending on the grade level.

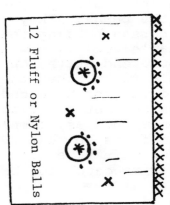

RUN RABBIT RUN

Three players are selected to be hunters and are placed in
center court, the remainder of the class is placed on a line
at one side of the court. On the signal, the players in the
line take off (staying in bounds) and attempt to run to the
other side of the court without getting hit with a fluff ball
The center players are allowed to throw 3 balls each on one
run. The other 6 fluff balls are ready to go. If a player
is hit, he/she sits down at the spot where he/she got hit and
becomes a hunter. He/she must stay on his/her bottom and not
move around, but he/she can tag players and then, they sit
down and become hunters. The last two players not hit or
tagged, become hunters.
VARIATION: Have the rabbits pull flags instead. Caught
players stand instead of sit.

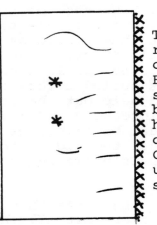

BRITISH BULLDOG

To begin, 2 players move to the center of the court, and the
rest of the players line up on one end or one side of the
court. When the players in the middle yell out "British
Bulldog," the other players try to run past them to the opposite ends of the court (field) without getting caught. To
be caught, a runner must be lifted off of the ground and
held long enough to yell "British Bulldog 1, 2, 3." The
catchers can plot and cooperate to catch larger players.
Caught players become center players and the game continues
until there are no side line players left. NOTE: Play until
side line players dwindle down to ____.

Primary Favorites

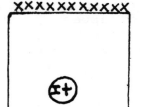

SPACEMAN/SPACEMAN

AREA: Gym or Playground. EQUIPMENT: None. PLAYERS: 20-30
"It" stands on a planet in outer space. From the line,
everyone chants, "Spaceman, Spaceman, may we chase you?" He/
she answers, "Yes, if you have on green." Then, only those
with green chase "It" around until one person tags him/her or
pulls his/her flag. (Say Spacegirl when appropriate).
Repeat with new "It" and change the color.

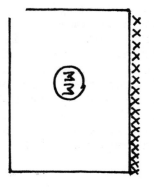

MAN FROM MARS

PLAYERS: Class. Object is to be the last one tagged.
Earthlings call, "Man from Mars, Man from Mars. Will you
take us to the stars?" Man from Mars replies, "Only if you
are wearing (color)." Those with the color called may walk
safely to other side. Players without the color run for the
other side and try to avoid getting tagged. Those tagged
join Man from Mars in center of the playing area.

SQUIRRELS IN THE TREES
AREA: M.P. Room or Blacktop. EQUIPMENT: None
A tree is formed by two players facing each other with hands
held or hands on each other's shoulders. A "Squirrel" is in
the center of each tree, and one or two extra squirrels are
outside. A signal to change is given as in musical chairs.
All squirrels move out of their trees to another, and the
extra players try to find trees. Only one squirrel is
allowed in a tree. To form a system of rotation, as each
squirrel moves into a tree, he/she changes places with one
of the two players forming the tree. NOTE: If you are in
the M.P. Room, you can have the squirrels skipping, etc. to
music. When the music goes off, all squirrels flee for the
trees.

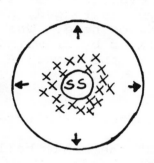

SPIDERS AND FLIES
Two players are selected to be spiders. The rest of the
players are flies. The job of the spiders is to encourage
the flies to come as close to the web (center circle) as
possible; then at a split second, they yell "trap." The
flies take off and attempt to get across the safety line
before their flags are pulled. If their flag gets pulled
before they cross the line, they become spiders and help
out the spiders. NOTE: The teacher can use the whistle
to set the trap.

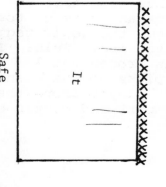

MOUSE TRAP
Children, in a large circle, join hands and raise their arms
high to make the mouse trap. A small group of the children
(mice) run through the trap. The teacher, who is part of
the circle, calls the signal "SNAP." When the circle
children hear the signal to snap the trap, they quickly
lower their arms. When the trap shuts, the mice inside
become part of the circle near the teachers. When all are
caught, new mice are named.

TOMMY TUCKER
AREA: Gym or Playground. EQUIPMENT: None. PLAYERS: 20
Tommy Tucker stands in the middle with all his gold and
silver around him. Players from the line chant, "We're on
Tommy Tucker's land, picking up gold and silver." As they
chant, they run up to Tommy and try to steal his gold without being tagged. If tagged, they must return the gold and
sit out until the next game starts. A new "It" is selected
from the one who picks up the most gold.

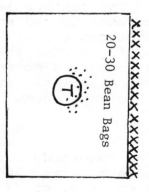

HILL DILL COME OVER THE HILL
AREA: Gym or Playground. EQUIPMENT: None. PLAYERS: 30
"It" chants from the center, "Hill Dill come over the hill,
I'll catch you if you're standing still." All children run
and "It" tries to tag them. If they're tagged, they must
help "It." Repeat the chant with all the people who got
tagged.

Tag Games

STUCK IN THE MUD

EQUIPMENT: 6 erasers, fluffballs, or 6 - 7" balls.
Six players are designated to be "IT" players. They all are
holding a ball. Their mission is to tag everyone that is
playing and stop all action. Once a player is tagged, he/she
must stand still with feet apart and hands on head. The remaining free players can free a tagged player by crawling
between their legs. Wham! They're back in the game. A
continuous exhausting tag game.

LINE TAG

AREA: Basketball Court. EQUIPMENT: 3 softballs, fluffballs, erasers, etc.
Players are spread out on lines throughout the basketball
court. Three players have objects in their hands. They are
the taggers. The other 27 players attempt to stay away from
them and not get tagged. "All" players must stay on lines.
All Lines! If a player is tagged, he has the object -
continuous play. NOTE: This is a great movement game with
music in the M.P. Room. Players will go a whole record.
Then rest, then play again with music. NOTE: Use 2 basketball courts side by side outside.

TEN SECOND TAG

AREA: Basketball size court. EQUIPMENT: 4 cones;
teacher needs a watch.
Half of the players are inside the court. The other half
is lined up and ready to go in the court. The teacher lets
one player in at a time. He/she has 10 seconds to tag someone. If the tagger does tag someone, the tagged player
exits out and "rewards" him/herself by jogging around the
court and getting in line. If 10 seconds go by and no one
is caught, the tagger exits and does the same. Lines turn
over rapidly. Tasks can be set up along the way - jump
rope - 2 jumps - 2 jumping jacks, etc.

BEAN BAG FREEZE TAG

Each player is given a bean bag to place on some body part
(directed by teacher); all on heads, shoulders, arms, etc.
Three people have an object, fluffball, deck ring, whiffle
ball, etc. These players are taggers; they also have on
bean bags. They chase players and try to hand them or touch
them with the object. If they do tag them, the newly tagged
players are "IT" players and are after everyone. Rule: If
a chased player drops his bean bag, he is frozen until
another player comes by and bends down, picks up the bean
bag and places it on him/her. If an "IT" player drops the
bean bag, he/she can put it back on body part and continue.

LAST FLAG PULLED

EQUIPMENT: Football flags
All players begin game wearing football flags. On "go,"
everyone begins pulling everyone else's flag. The last
player to have a flag, wins. NOTE: On each pulled flag,
the flag must be handed to the teacher. Everyone is in
until the last flag is pulled. VARIATION: Let players
keep the pulled flags and put them back into pockets. Continuous play - Aerobic - End the game on a recess.

BLOB TAG

Players are scattered in the defined area. Two players are
holding hands and are the "initial blob." The "blob" runs
around tagging other players with outside hands. As players
are tagged, they become part of the blob by joining hands.
Only outside players tag other players.

BACK TO BACK TAG

An uneven number of players is needed for this tag game.
Players stand back to back with one "out" player. The
teacher yells, "Back to back" or blows a whistle, and all
players scramble for a new back to back person. The "out"
player also scrambles to get back to back with someone. The
remaining player is the "out" player for this round. The
object of the game is to not be the "out" player.

SIAMESE TAG

EQUIPMENT: Super rubber bands, balls, or erasers
The game begins with everyone paired up with inner tube
strips from an old car, holding the legs together on the
inside, just below the knee. One pair of players is holding
a ball, and they are the "it" players. They attempt to tag
other pairs of players with the ball. When they tag a pair,
the new pair accepts the object and becomes the "it" players.
Continuous play. VARIATION: Players wear bands on upper
arms.

HUG TAG

AREA: Basketball size court. EQUIPMENT: 2 soft objects
Play begins with everyone standing by himself. Two players
have a soft object, fluffball, etc. The teacher calls out
"3's." Everyone must get into 3's before the taggers can
catch a player and tag him/her. If a player gets tagged, he/
she becomes "it." The teacher may call 2's, 4's, 5's, etc.
The new "it" players have the objects.

HOOK ON TAG "LOOSE CABOOSE"

Teams of 5 or 6 players are designated. They are spread out
around the court. The first player steps out and faces his
line. The line is one player behind another, hooked on with
each player having hands on hips of player in front. The
last player may have a flag sticking out of his/her pocket.
The object for the team is to protect the last player by
staying hooked up but moving around so that the free player
cannot grab the flag. VARIATION: Team hook on flag - the
whole team is hooked up, only the end player has a flag.
Teams try to collect as many flags from the other teams as
possible. VARIATION: Circle hook on tag - all players
except one are holding hands in a small circle. One circle
player has a flag in his/her pocket. Loose player attempts
to get flag.

The game begins with players standing in 2's facing each other. One player is the "out" player (no partner). The object of the game is to always be paired up and to not become the out player. The teacher decides whether or not he/she needs to play. When the teacher calls out, "People to People," everyone pairs up with someone else, and the out player tries to pair up - a new out player exists. In between the call, "People to People," the teacher may say - Toe to Toe, Knee to Knee, Back to Back, Side to Side, Finger to Finger, etc. Then the change call, "People to People." Continue.

SQUAT TAG

The game is played like ordinary tag with the exception that players may free themselves from being tagged by assuming a squatting position. While the same player is "IT" however, they may do this once. Use a small object for the "IT" player to carry. Fluffballs, erasers, etc. can be used.

CHINESE TAG

The "IT" player tries to tag any of the other players on an awkward spot such as the knee, ankle, elbow, etc. The new "IT" player must hold his/her hand on that spot while chasing the other players; the other players must hold their hands on the same spot while being chased.

ELBOW TAG

The game begins with everyone standing in 2's with elbows locked together and <u>outside</u> elbows on <u>hips</u> except for the "out" player. When the action begins, the "out" player tries to hook on to the outside elbows while couples avoid the "out" player. When he/she hooks on, the player on the other side becomes the "out" player. Continuous play.

LAST COUPLE

Players are lined up by couples in a column formation with an "IT" standing at the head of the column. He has his back to the column. He calls, "Last couple out." The object of the game is to have the last couple separate and rejoin beyond the place where "IT" is standing without being tagged by him. If "IT" tags either of the two, that person becomes "IT." The old "IT" joins the remaining player as his partner, and the pair go to the head of the line. If the couple is able to join hands without being tagged, they take places at the head of the column, and "IT" takes a try at the next couple. "IT" is not permitted to look back and cannot start his chase until the separated couple comes up even with him on both sides. VARIATION: The game can be played by partners who have inside hands joined.

THREE DEEP

A runner and chaser are chosen. One-half of the remaining children form a circle, facing in. Each of the other children stands behind one of the circle players, forming a double circle formation with all facing in. The chaser tries to tag the runner, who can escape by taking a position in front of any pair of players. This forms a 3-deep combination, from which the game gets its name. The outer player the 3 now is the runner. When the chaser tags the runner, the positions are reversed. Game becomes more interesting frequent changes are made. It may be well to limit running to halfway around the circle. In no case, should the runner leave the immediate circle area.

This game stresses listening, following directions, and quick movements performed with control. Four of your students are selected to be "Fish Gobblers." Each Fish Gobbler is given an object to carry in one hand - eraser, fluffball, sport foam ball. Fish Gobblers follow the same rules and directions that the other players follow until the teacher calls, "Fish Gobbler." At that time, the Fish Gobblers attempt to tag as many players as possible before they can get into Fish Gobbler position, which is "body flat on the floor and connected to at least one other person." Players tagged while not in position are sent to the brig. Players in the brig perform 10 sit ups, 10 push ups, 10 jumping jacks and they are back in the game. Other commands given by the teacher are:

Shipwreck - run to the right wall

Iceberg - freeze

Dive - hit the deck

Man Overboard - player in 2's; one player on hands and knees, the other with one knee on partner's back - searching

Man in the Galley - players in 3's, flat on backs, legs in air with feet touching

Fog Horn - standing straight and tall, turning around, making fog horn noises

Swim - specific instructions, strokes, backstroke, etc.

Walk the Plank - 3 steps, jump up, then sink to the floor

Storm - run to the left wall

Torpedo - run in a scattered pattern around the room

Drop the Anchor - sit

REVERSE TAG

An even number of players are needed for this game. Players stand about one yard apart while facing each other. One player is designated to be the chaser and another, the chased player. The chaser begins chasing the chased player. When the chased player gets tired or is about to be tagged, he/she steps between two players. The player that is now facing the chased player's back becomes the chaser and the game reverses. Note: Use more than one team of chasers and chased players.

HIT THE DECK TAG

AREA: Coned off grass area. EQUIPMENT: 6 - 7" balls, erasers, or visible objects.
Six players are designated to be "IT" players. They are all holding a visible object. Their mission is to tag everyone that is playing and stop all the action. A player can keep from being tagged by hitting the deck and turning upside down with arms and legs pointed upward. Tagged players hit the deck and remain on stomach. Upside down players can get up and run anytime. Any free player can tag any stomach player and free him/her. Continuous play.

Relays

BROOM RELAYS
EQUIPMENT: 6 Brooms
Five teams of 6 are lined up. Runners can ride the broom
singularly or in 2's or 3's around a cone and back. Runner
can sweep objects down and back with the broom. Runners ca
hold the broom in different positions or balance the broom
down and back.

BOWLING RELAYS
EQUIPMENT: 6 Balls
Teams of 5 are lined up. The first player runs to a line
about 20' to 30' from start, turns, and rolls ball back to
next player who waits until ball crosses the starting line.
He/she takes off and does the same. The first team to have
everyone across the line, wins.

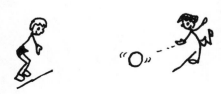

OVER 'N OVER RELAYS
EQUIPMENT: 6 Balls. TOTAL MOVEMENT RELAY.
The first player passes the ball over head and everyone doe
the same. As soon as a player passes the ball, he/she immediately peels off and becomes the end of the line. "Pas:
'n Peel" - "Pass 'n Peel." The whole team moves backward and
must cross the finish line. VARIATION: Under n Under.

THREE PEOPLE SIDE STEP RELAYS - AEROBICS
Ten teams of three are placed in the center of the basketb
court. Each team is holding hands. On "go," all teams bee
side stepping to the line on the edge of the basketball
court. Touch a foot outside, side step all the way back
across as a unit. Touch a foot outside, come back to the
other side. Pre-set number of lines to cross 8 - 1 - line
Good practice for side step test and endurance.

LONG DISTANCE RELAYS
EQUIPMENT: 6 Batons or Erasers
Players are lined up. The first runners in line go all the
way out to the fence (one hand on fence). The second runners go out about half way to the fence. The third runner
in line start the relay with an object in hand. The start
runner carries the object to the half way runner and stays
The half way runner carries the object to the fence runner
and stays. The fence runner carries the object to start a
passes it off to first player in line. The first player
takes off. The relay is run until everyone is back in pla
The starting runner carries to the fence runner and stays.
The fence runner carries it back to start. The starting
player takes off. The relay is run until everyone is back
in starting position.

JUNK RELAYS
EQUIPMENT: 10 Hoops - Junk - Ball, Ruler, Tape, Pencil, E
Six teams of 5 in a line. A hoop, tire, or mat is placed
directly in front of each team, and another is placed at t
end of the relay area. 4, 5, 6, 7 objects are placed in t
hoops directly in front of each team. The runners must ru
pick up all the objects, take them to the far hoop, set th
inside, run back, tag the next runner. The next runner ru
to far hoop, picks up junk, brings it back to close hoop,
tags next runner.

TRAVEL RELAYS

EQUIPMENT: 15 Hoops, 6 Jump Ropes, 6 Bean Bags or Tires,
6 Balls
Six teams of 5 line up. Three hoops or tires are layed out
about 12 yards apart in front of each team. A jump rope is
placed in first hoop, a bean bag in the second, and a ball
in the third. The first runner takes off, runs to first tire
and picks up the jump rope, jump ropes to the next tire, puts
rope inside, picks up bean bag and puts on head, fast walks
to next tire, puts bean bag inside, picks up ball, dribbles
back to tire one, puts ball inside and runs back and tags
next runner. Definitely Reinforcement.

BLINDFOLD RELAYS

EQUIPMENT: 15 Blindfolds
Players stand in lines of 6. Players then pair up within the
lines. One player has blindfold on, one is the guide. The
first two players in each line take off; the guide talks to,
but doesn't touch blindfolded player. They go down around
the cone and back, tag next two players, and relay continues.
Player reverse positions.

STEPPING STONE RELAYS

EQUIPMENT: 16 Mats or Newspapers
Teams of 4 are lined up across the basketball court. Each
team has two mats. The first player lays a mat down, steps
on it, sets the next mat down, steps on it, picks up pre-
vious stepped on mat, sets it down, steps on it until he/she
has worked way to line across the court. He/she picks up
mats, runs back, gives them to next player. This is continuous until all 4 players have participated.

COOPERATIVE RELAYS

TOTAL MOVEMENT RELAYS
Each team of 6 players is grouped in a small circle with one
player in the middle and 5 players holding hands. On "go,"
the team takes off with middle player running and staying
right in the middle; one person on team must cross the line,
then the whole team takes off for starting line. When starting line is crossed by one player, the team exchanges the
player in the middle and takes off again. Continue until
everyone has been in the middle.

TRAIN RELAYS

Each team of 5 players is lined up. All participants have
their hands on the shoulders of the runner in front of them.
On "go," the team takes off and circles the cone and returns
to cross the starting line and circle the cone on the starting line. As the team is circling the cone, the lead
runner steps out and joins the back of the line and the
team relays again. This procedure takes place until everyone is back in starting position on the starting line.
VARIATION: Use a jump rope for team members to hand on to
instead of using shoulders.
NOTE: Wide lanes for turning - short distance.

OTHER COOPERATIVE RELAYS

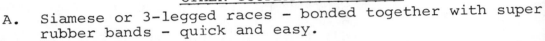

A. Siamese or 3-legged races - bonded together with super rubber bands - quick and easy.

B. Joined hands or hands both holding a baton.

C. Wheelbarrow.

D. Chariot Relays - 3 people. Two players join inside hands; the third player holds onto outside hands of joined players. Two chariots make a team. Have a lot of space for turning lines. Run and rest. Run and res

E. Sedan Relays - 3 people - two to carry, one to ride. To form a seat for the carry, two players face each other. Each grabs his/her own left wrist with right hand. The open hand now grasps the partner's wrist. The person carried sits on the seat and puts his/her hands around the necks of the carriers.

MOTOR SKILL REINFORCEMENT RELAYS

EQUIPMENT: Cards

Teams of 5 are lined up. A set of cards is placed on a ma face down about 5' in front of line. The first runners ru out, take a card, and perform those motor skills down and back. The card might say, "Run Down, Skip Back." Run off one set for each relay line - 6 sets.

CARD POSSIBILITIES

Run Down Skip Back	Run Very Cool Down Skip Back	Run Backward Down Zig-Zag Run Back	Shake N Run Down Gallop Back
Run Tall Down Run Short Back	Side Step Down Jump Back	Run Backward Down Leap Back	Skip Down Skip Backward Back
Run Stiff Legged Down Run Stiff Legged Backward Back	Zig-Zag Run Down Leap Back	Slide Down Hop Back	Gallop Down Zig-Zag Run Back
Hop Down Run Back	Gallop all of the way	Slide Left Side Only Down and Back	Slide Right Side Only Down and Back
Slide - Change Sides Slide - Change Sides Down and Back	Hop Right Foot Down Hop Left Foot Back	Zig-Zag Run All of the Way Down and Back	Leap Down and Back
Cool Run Down and Back	Imagining Dribble as you Run Down and Back	Skip Down Gallop Back	Leap Down Gallop Back
Slide Down Skip Back	Run Down Slide Back	Zig-Zag Down Run Back	Slide Down Leap Back	Zig-Zag Skip Down Run Back

NOTE: Run cards off on tag board or poster board. Use the old hand crank ditto machine that no one else uses.

A. Players stand in lines. They run to end; some type o matching activity is at the end of relay - Homonyms, Synonyms, Antonyms, Math facts, etc. Make sure that they have them in mind. It must be reinforcement.

CHARIOTS OF FIRE RELAYS

Each team of 5 or 6 players is placed on the starting line in a circle. All players are facing outward and holding hands except for the driver who is facing inward and holding hands. He/she is positioned at the back of the circle. On "go," the team takes off, circles the cone and returns to circle the cone on the starting line. As the team is circling the cone, the chariot driver changes places with someone else. This procedure takes place until every player has had an opportunity to be the driver. The first team that crosses the finish line, wins.
NOTE: Wide lanes for turning - short distance.

PONY EXPRESS RELAYS

EQUIPMENT: 4 Pinnies, Batons or Erasers
This relay should incorporate the perimeter of your grass area. Teams are first lined up in groups of 6. Then, moved by number - all ones, twos, etc. - to specific areas around the edge of the grass area. The first runners all have pinnies on and batons or erasers in hand. On "go," they take off, run to number 2 runners, take pinnies off, put them on number 2 players, hand batons off and stay there. Number 2 players run to number 3 and do the same. When everyone is back in starting position, the relay is over.

KANGAROO RELAYS

The first player in each line holds the ball between his/ her knees with pressure. The player jumps forward retaining control of the ball, around the turning point, and jumps back to the head of the line where he gives the ball to the next player who repeats. If the ball drops out, it must be replaced on the spot.

STUNT AND ANIMAL RELAYS

Lame Dog	Lame Kangaroo	Crab Walk	Bear Walk
Frog Hop	Ostrich Walk	Alligator Crawl	
Seal Walk	Etc.		

Large Group Game Formats

THREE STATION STEAL THE BACON

EQUIPMENT: Variety of equipment adds interest.
1. Brooms - balls
2. 2 foot sticks - pop cans
3. Hands (paddles) - balls
4. Feet - cans
5. Plastic bats - wiffle balls
6. Ping pong paddles - bean bags

Participants are divided into teams of 5 or 6. This division of students provides for total class involvement. Specific skills can be worked into the game. Example: Ball in center; players run out, use their feet to dribble ball back across the line (soccer skill). Each team on a side is numbered from 1 to 5 or 1 to 6. The teacher will call one number. If the player's number is called, he/she then hurries to the center, picks up the piece of equipment for pushing and tries to push the floor object back across his/her home base line before the players from the opposing team can get to it. For added interest, rotate the groups to the next set of objects after each number has been called at least once. NOTE: This format is great for setting up 3 small groups of crab soccer.

TASK STEAL THE BACON

EQUIPMENT: 30 pocket flags, 4 hula hoops, bike tires, wastebaskets, cones, 8 flags to be used as objects for players to take after teacher drops them on the wastebasket. Teams of 15 are placed along the sidelines. Directions are given to each team in regard to the direction in which they are supposed to take the flag and run. Each team member has a football flag placed in his/her back pocket or equitable place. The teacher is holding about 8 flags in his/her hand. He/she tells each team that 2 players will come out each time that a flag is dropped on the trash can, and each player coming out will try to pick up the flag and head for his/her designated end of the court. The player who does not get the flag will try to pull the flag that is in the opponent's pocket before he/she gets across the line. The player with the flag in hand must perform some (one) kind of task before moving across the line.

1. Go through the vertical hoop; 2. Jump with both feet in the flat hoop; 3. Perform some type of stunt or, 4. Place the flag cleanly down on the trash can with one hand and pick it up with the other. Then cross the line. Any 3 or 4 tasks can be made by the teacher. Point values are assigned to each task. Students get so involved that everyone soon forgets about the score. The teacher does not warn the students as he/she drops the flags; they must keep moving into the cones and be aware. Turn lines over every minute. Return flags to teacher and players immediately.

POSSIBILITIES

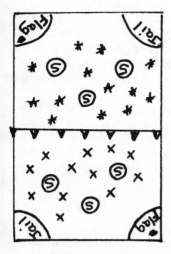

FIELD ACTIVITY

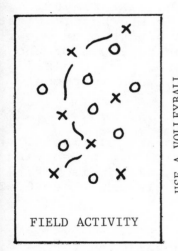

FIELD ACTIVITY

USE A VOLLEYBALL

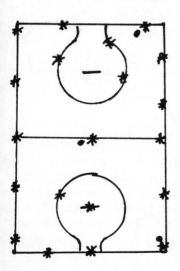

CAPTURE THE FLAG

EQUIPMENT: 6 hoops, 2 flags, 4 long turning ropes,
30 football flags
Teams are divided (2) equally. They line up across from
each other at the center of the field. The objective is to
capture your opponent's flag and bring it back across the
center line without getting your own personal flag pulled.
If any player is caught (tagged), he/she is sent to jail.
Jail Release: A player can be released from jail if another
player can make it safely into the jail area. Only one released player per time. The two players step out of bounds
and run back up the sideline to the center line and resume
play. Football flags are returned by the teacher.
Safety Areas: Inside of jail - flag area and hoops. Only
one player can be inside a hoop at a time.
Flag: The captured flag must stay in plain sight at all
times.
NOTE: Encourage children to plan a strategy.
NOTE: The use of football flags for all players increases
interest. When flags are pulled, keep them yourself until
students are released from jail - saves arguments.

SPEEDBALL/FOOTBALL

Players are divided into 2 equal teams. All players are
wearing football flags. One team is wearing pinnies. One
team begins with the ball about 1/3 of the way up the field.
The objective is to get the ball across your opponent's goal
line by running or passing the ball without (1) letting the
ball drop to the ground; (2) getting your flag pulled when
you have the ball; (3) getting intercepted. All three items
result in a turnover, and the ball goes to the other team on
the spot. Teams must pass to at least 3 people before they
can cross their opponent's goal line. If a team intercepts
on the one footline, the ball must be passed to 3 people
(minimum) before a touchdown can be made.
VARIATION: Run 2 games at the same time. Use short fields
for success and motivation. Four teams of 8 - referee both
games.
VARIATION: Play this game with frisbees, or scoops and
tennis balls.

COURT LINE TAG

Players are spread out on line throughout the basketball
court. Three players have objects in their hands. They
are the taggers. The other 27 players attempt to stay away
from them and not get tagged. "All" players must stay on
lines. All Lines! If a player is tagged, he/she gets the
object - continuous play.
NOTE: This is a great movement game with music in M.P.
Room. Players will continue play until the record stops.
Then rest. Then play again with music. Outside play -
extend game to two courts side by side.

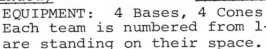

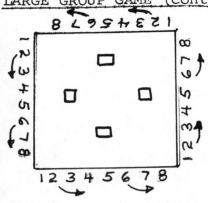

EQUIPMENT: 4 Bases, 4 Cones
Each team is numbered from 1-8 consecutively. Players
are standing on their space. The teacher calls out 2's and
6's. All 2's and 6's take off, relay around the four corners and run to center through their own vacated space and
end on the base that is designated to be the team base.
First player to end earns 4 points for his/her team. Fi-
nishing teams receive 3, 2, and 1 point accordingly.
VARIATION: Players can sit around edge and the first player
back in place, wins.
VARIATION: Balance on one foot combatives - hop in - make
opponents put their other foot down. Use the ball to push
opponents.
VARIATION: Star Wars Dodgeball. Use the rebound nets and
about 12 nylon or fluff balls. Play the same rules as in
Wastebasket Dodgeball.

HOOP BALL

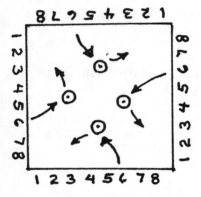

EQUIPMENT: Red Balls, Four Hoops
Four teams are divided equally. A hoop and a ball are desig
nated for each team as seen in diagram. Players in lines ar
assigned permanent numbers. The teacher calls a number (6);
all number 6's race out and take the ball from the hoop and
race to number 1 position and hand the ball to #1. He/she,
in turn, hands the ball to #2 and on to the last player.
The last player races with the ball back to the hoop. First
team to finish wins the round. All players move over one
space as players are racing out to get the ball out of the
hoop. After the player in the last position puts the ball
in the hoop, he/she runs over and assumes the number one
position. Resume Play.

STRIKE BALL DODGEBALL

Players are arbitrarily placed around a square or circle.
Circle players attempt to put center players out by serving
the ball as in a volleyball serve. When a player is hit,
the striker exchanges places with the hit player. Keep 6 or
7 balls going. A self-contained game.

BOWLING DODGEBALL

Use the same rules as in Strike Ball Dodgeball, only the
circle players bowl the balls at center players.

PINBALL DODGEBALL

Use the same rules as Strike Ball Dodgeball, only the
circle players turn around and shoot the ball between their
legs at center players.

GUARD 'N GANGSTER DODGEBALL

Players are arbitrarily placed around the square or circle.
Center players are hooked together - the player in back
places his/her hands on waist of front player. Circle
players attempt to hit Gangster (back player); when Gangster
is hit, the Guard becomes the Gangster, and the Gangster
goes to the edge of square or circle. The player who hit
the Gangster comes in and plays in front of Gangster as the
Guard.

**☀☀ GUARD N GANGSTER

☀☀☀ DONKEY DODGEBALL

DONKEY DODGE

Play the same as Guard 'n Gangster, only 3 players are hooked
together instead of 2. The object of circle players is to
hit the tail or last player. Rotate as in above game.

PIN BOUNDARY BALL

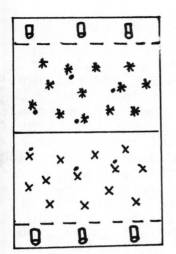

EQUIPMENT: 7' Balls (Soccer or Volleyballs), Tennis
Ball Cans
Players are divided into 2 teams. Each team begins with
3, 4, 5, 6, 7 balls. On signal, members of each team attempt
to roll the ball across their opponent's end zone area. De-
fending players cannot stop a ball in the end zone area.
SCORING: 1 point is scored each time that a ball crosses the
end zone area. 3 points are scored if a pin is knocked down.
Team plays until "X" amount of pins are knocked down.
NOTE: (1) Teams can continually set pins up and have continuous play. The M.P. Room is a much better place to play
as there are walls to stop the balls. Emphasize "Bowling"
safety. (2) Tennis ball cans can be used in place of bowling
pins. (3) A throwing game can be developed if sportfoam
balls are used. Use 10 bowling pins or tennis ball cans.
Some of them set up on wastebaskets.

NEWSPAPER SWAT

EQUIPMENT: 6 Wastebaskets, 6 Swatters (rolled up newspapers
that are taped with masking tape), 30 Mats for outer circle
players
Players form a circle; six players are designated to be center players and move to center area and sit down on a wastebasket that has been turned upside down. A swatter is
placed beside the can. Each circle player should be standing
on a small mat with no extra mats around the circle. Ex:
24 circle players - 24 mats. Players number off from 1 -
30 including center players. Players keep the <u>same number</u>
throughout the game, but do not keep the same space. The
teacher calls out 5 or 6 random numbers such as 6, 19, 4,
11, 2, and 27 and says "go." These six people must run and
exchange positions before the wastebasket players can pick
up a swatter and swat someone on the <u>seat</u> lightly. The
swatters drop the newspaper on the swat, and the swatted
players pick up the newspapers and attempt to re-swat any
player in the circle who does not have a newspaper. Everyone gets in place; all mats are covered with players, and
the teacher calls six new numbers, says "go;" play resumes.
NOTE: (1) It is very important to players for the teacher
to check off numbers evenly. (2) Players really enjoy this
activity. (3) Two games of 15 players each can be played
side by side with 3 wastebasket players in each circle.

KEEP TRACK OF NUMBERS

WASTEBASKET DODGEBALL

A circle is formed. Six players are sent to the center with
a wastebasket. The balls are given to the players on the
perimeter of the playing area. They begin throwing the balls
at the center players. The center players use the wastebaskets to bunt the balls away. When a player is hit, the
thrower takes his place in the circle. Continuous play.
Hold the wastebasket so that the bottom is facing out and
toward the circle.
NOTE: This game could be one large game with 6 players in
the center with wastebaskets, or two games with 3 wastebaskets and 3 throwers. Six throwers - 6 dodgers at all
times.
Sportfoam balls are the greatest! Nobody gets hurt!
"Kids like the sound of the sportfoam balls thumping the
wastebaskets."

RUN IN TO GET THE BALL

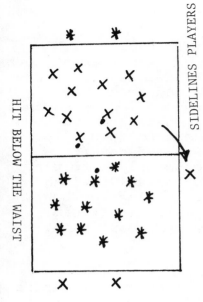

HIT BELOW THE WAIST

SIDELINES PLAYERS

DOUBLE DODGEBALL

EQUIPMENT: 2 or 3 Large Red Balls
Players are divided into two equal teams with two goalies
on each team, placed at the opposite end of the court. One
goalie on each end starts the game by throwing the ball at
the players in front of him/her. Players are out when hit
by the ball on any part of the body or clothes. Players are
out when they move one foot over any line. When the first
person is out, he/she becomes the goalie and thus replaces
the starting goalie who then goes into the game. After each
member is out, he/she replaces a goalie until all the starting goalies are in the game. After all starting goalies are
in the game, the players become goalies as they are hit or
play the sidelines and remain outside. If a team member
attempts to catch the ball and drops it, he/she is out, but
can then throw the ball at the opposite team from the sideline. If the ball hits one or more team members and is not
caught before hitting the ground, both are out. Both teams
can have side goalies. When all members are hit and out,
the game is over and the team with the last player left in a
court is declared the winner. This can be changed to "X"
number left to end game.

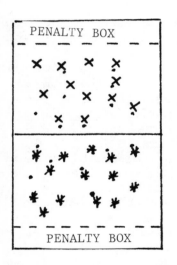

PENALTY BOX

PENALTY BOX

BOMBARDMENT

EQUIPMENT: 20 Nylon Stocking Balls or 20 Fluff Balls
Teams are divided equally (2). They line up across from
each other. The back 2 yards of each court is off limits
unless a player is retrieving a ball or is in the penalty
box for getting hit with a ball. Players are encouraged to
run up as close to the center as they can with a ball, throw
it, and hit another player on the opposite team and not get
hit themselves. If a player is hit, he then goes to the
penalty box. The team with the most players still involved,
wins. NOTE: Games should not exceed 2 minutes in order to
get everyone back into play as soon as possible.
VARIATION: (1) You go back in when someone is out; (2) Set
up 3 or 4 tennis ball cans in center of each court. No
guarding the can. When all are knocked down, the other team
wins. No one goes out.

THROW FROM BEHIND THE LINE

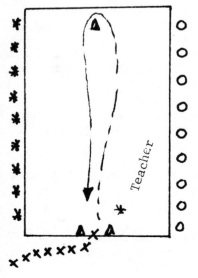

Teacher

ROUND TRIP DODGEBALL

EQUIPMENT: Cones, 6 Sportfoam Balls
Players are divided into 3 teams. Each team makes its turn
in the "X" position. "X" players take off one at a time,
circle the cone, and return to the line. "*" and "o" players let the balls fly under teacher direction: throw underhand, overhand, side arm, hit below the waist, etc. Running
player must make it back and forth within 10 seconds or adjusted time. A time limit keeps the game moving. Time
limit optional. Runs are scored when players make it safely
(without getting hit) around the cone and back to the line.
Teacher says - only underhand throw or side arm, or overhand, below waist, etc.
NOTE: (1) Non-threatening balls are a must; (2) One point
can be awarded for making it down even if runner gets hit
going back; 2 points for a round trip. If runners get hit
on the way down, the teacher can keep the runners with him/
her and send them all back at once to save time.

CROWN THE KING

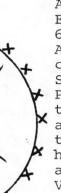

AREA: M.P. Room, Grass, or Blacktop
EQUIPMENT: 6 Bike Tires, 6 Sportfoam Balls (8½") and 6 Tennis Ball Cans
A large circle is formed; 6 bike tires are placed in the center of the circle with a tennis ball can in each tire. Six players are selected to come in and protect the cans. Protectors aren't allowed to step inside the tires. Protectors protect only one can. Six balls are distributed among the players on the outer circle. Players begin throwing balls at cans while protectors, without using hands, protect their own cans. The person who knocks down a can, replaces the protector. Continuous play.
VARIATION: Break the game into 2 smaller circles and play 2 games with students playing at 2 levels.
NOTE: (1) Sportfoam balls are the greatest! Nobody gets hurt. (2) If one big circle is used - 6 tires, 6 cans, 6 balls - keeps your students hustling.

BUDDY SPUD

STAY INSIDE OF CIRCLE

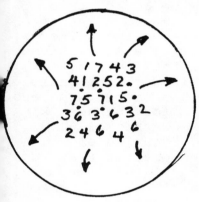

NOTE CARD 1 - 7

FOR TEACHER

EQUIPMENT: Cones for Circle, 4 or 5 - 7" Balls, Clip Board, Note Card marked 1-7
Have players gather around you in the center of a large marked circle. Players are numbered from 1-7 with 4 players having the same number. 1111 - 2222 ... EXPLANATION: Have the 1's throw the balls up; you call out 6. The four 6's retrieve the balls while all other players scatter to the edge of the circle. The 6's then bowl the ball toward the scattered players. The scattered players must leave both feet on the ground while they attempt to dodge the ball. Dodging players can turn feet on edge; they just cannot lift a foot off of the ground while they are dodging a ball that has been bowled toward them. If a player is hit, he/she takes a point for his/her designated team. If the bowler misses everyone, he/she takes a point for his/her designated team. Tally scores and start again with the 6's tossing up the balls.
NOTE: (1) The team with the fewest points at the end of the game, wins. (2) Have students balance on one foot, throwers close eyes - whatever. Bowl the ball.

BATTLE ROYAL

CALL TWO NUMBERS

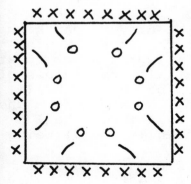

EQUIPMENT: 8 Deck Rings, 8 Sportfoam Balls
Four teams of equal number of players line up on 4 sides of court. Each team has a sideline as its home base. Players on each team are numbered correspondingly. A ball is placed on each deck ring. When 2 numbers are called, opposing players come out, take balls, and attempt to hit opposing players with their balls. The players on the line also retrieve balls and throw them at opposing team players inside. Players may block thrown balls with the ball that they are holding, or catch a thrown ball. Players must stay inside of court; any player hit must go to the sideline. The last player in scores a point for his/her team. Set a point limit (optional).
VARIATION: Crab Soccer - Use 3 beach balls or large red rubber balls; 4 teams as usual. Call 3 numbers (3, 6, 2). Twelve players come out in crab walk position and kick balls from center across anyone's goal line. Players on sides are in crab walk position trying to kick in balls.

Kick Ball Game Formats and Variations

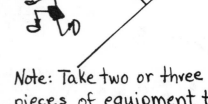

Note: Take two or three pieces of equipment to the game - when one ball is out of play, pitch in the next.

The Homerun Rule: The kicker must make a homerun before the players in the field perform their designated task with the ball.

Area: Black top or Grass.

Games designed to bring more involvement: Kicking, Running, Throwing, Dodging, Catching,

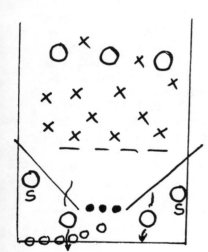

HOOPLA KICKBALL - DODGEBALL

Teams are divided (2) equally; one team is up to kick, the other team is out in the field. The object of this game is to score safely.

1. The ball is placed down on "Home Plate." The kicker kicks the ball into the field of players. The kicker then runs to one of the 3 hoops at the end of the field or "sticks" in a side hoop. If he/she is hit with the ball, he/she is out. The kicker must remain in a hoop at the end of the field or a side hoop by home plate for the next kick. A player cannot run down and back on his own kick.
2. A caught fly ball results in an out, "your rule."
3. If hoops at either end are full, everyone, at that end, must run.
4. Several outs can be made in one turn.
5. The last kicker must attempt to run both ways.
6. Safety Hoop - if a kicker kicks a weak kick, he can run sideways to the safety hoop and go down field on a strong kick by someone else. "Built in Success."
7. Hoops that are nearest the ball are to be used for players to pick up and put over their body before they cross the line on their return trip.

NOTE: If the teacher uses 3 balls, the ball out in the fiel can become a "dead" ball and a new one can be used to keep the game going while the other ball is being rolled in.

LONG BASE KICK - DODGEBALL

Divide the players into 2 equal teams. Up players can kick the ball and run to first or first and back home. Running rule: Players can stay at first until 3 players stack up at first; then everyone must run on the next kick regardless of how good or bad the kick is. Players can be put out by (1) first base being tagged by a player with the ball before the kicker-runner gets there, (2) being hit by a thrown ball below the waist between the long base and home or (3) being tagged with the ball while running.

NOTE: Four runs could be scored on one kick. Three outs could be made on one kick or play. Encourage field players to throw the ball carefully to hit the runner. Change sides after 3 outs. Use 10" Red Ball.

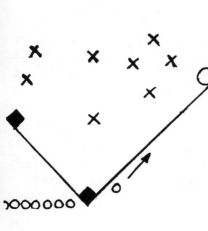

KICKBALL (Continued)

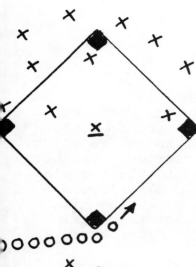

BEAT THE BALL

Divide the players into 2 equal teams. Play the rule of Home Run Kickball. The kicker kicks the pitched ball into the field of play. He/she then runs around all the bases before a member of the opposing team can retrieve the ball, step on a base, and throw the ball to other base players who, in turn, step on a base. The ball is thrown to all bases. Four players must handle the ball before the final base is tagged.

NOTE: Keep 2 balls in the game to avoid delays. Have all players kick before changing sides. Count runs, not outs.

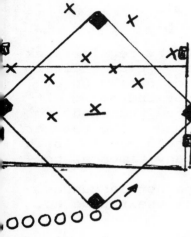

KICKBALL BASKETBALL

Divide the players into 2 equal teams. Play the rule of Home Run Kickball. The kicker kicks the pitched ball into the field of play. He/she then runs around all the bases before the opposing team can retrieve the ball and make a basket in any basketball hoop on the court. There could be as few as one basketball hoop or as many as six to use. If the runner runs around all bases before a basket is made, he/she scores one run.

NOTE: Keep 2 balls in game to avoid delays. Have all players kick before changing sides. Count runs, not outs.

VARIATION: Players must pass or dribble the ball. (Make adjustments with base length.)

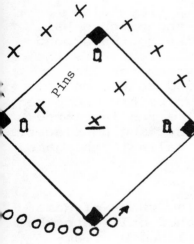

HIT THE PIN KICKBALL

Divide into 2 equal teams. Play the rules of Home Run Kickball. The kicker kicks the ball into the field of play and runs around all of the bases before players on the opposing team can pass the ball around and knock all the bowling pins down. The order of hitting the pins is not important. Keep the same team up until everyone has had a chance to kick. Count the runs, not the outs. Set pins inside of bases so that runners will not get tangled up with the pins.

NOTE: Emphasize teamwork. Three people must touch the ball while knocking the pins down. Keep 2 balls in game to avoid delays when one ball is out of play. Adjust success by changing bases and pins. (Optional pin at home plate.)

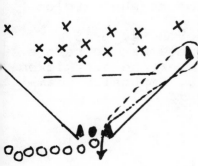

GOAL BALL

Teams are divided (2). Team B is placed on the field behind an imaginary boundary. They must wait there until the ball is kicked. The bases are set up as foul lines and are also goals for the kicker to run around when he/she kicks the ball. A kicker from Team A kicks the ball into fair territory and then runs around one of the bases and back through the goals before Team B can collectively kick the ball between the goals for one point.

SCORING: One point is allowed for each goal. Three outs and you change sides. A goal is allowed if any member of the team in field touches the ball with his/her hands.

VARIATION: Let everyone kick. Just count the runs, then change sides.

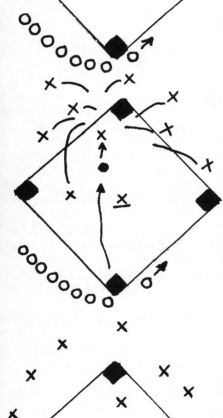

KICKBALL (Continued)

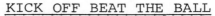

KICK OFF BEAT THE BALL

Divide players into 2 equal teams. Play the rules of
Home Run Kickball. The kicker kicks the teed football
into the field of play and then attempts to run to all
the bases before a player in the field retrieves the ball
and throws it to another player and then to all the players on the field, (players stand still). All players
must handle the ball. Have all players on a team kick
before changing sides. Count the runs, not the outs.
Fly balls that are caught cannot be counted as outs;
decide before you begin playing.
NOTE: Keep 2 balls teed up to speed up play.

MARATHON KICKBALL

Divide the players into 2 equal teams. Play regular kickball rules, except that teams do not change places after
3 outs. They change places after 3, 4, or 5 minutes of
play. Set the limit. Count the runs, not the outs. It
is the job of the up team to stay organized and ready to
kick. The teacher has 3 balls at the mound. The teacher's
job is to keep pitching the balls after outs and fouls in
order to turn the kicking line over as many times as possible within the time limit.
NOTE: As soon as the time is up, the teacher announces
the score, and then the other team begins their time up.

LINE IT UP KICKBALL

Divide the players into two equal teams. Play rules
of Home Run Kickball. The kicker kicks the pitched ball
into the field of play. He/she then tries to run around
all the bases before a player in the field retrieves the
ball, stands still, and all of his/her teammates line up
behind him/her and pass the ball over head to the end of
the line. If the runner makes a home run before the other
team can line up and pass back the ball, a run is scored.
NOTE: Let everyone on a team kick before changing places.
Count the runs, not the outs. Keep two balls in the game
to avoid delays.

DANISH ROUNDER KICKBALL

Divide players into two equal teams. Play rules of Home
Run Kickball. The kicker kicks the pitched ball into the
field of play. He then runs around his lined up teammates as many times as he can before a player in the
field can retrieve the ball, throw it to another player,
have that player throw it to another, and then tag home
plate. The runner scores a run each time he/she circles
his/her lined up teammates.
NOTE: The ball must be touched by either 3, 4, or 5
players in the field before it comes home. Decide before
the game. Keep the same team up until everyone has kicked
the ball. Count the runs, not the outs. Emphasize teamwork. Keep two balls in the game to avoid delays.

Non-Competitive Games and Activities

WHO IS THE KILLER OR THE WINKING GAME

A card is passed face down to each player from the referee. The referee states to the team which card is the Killer's Card. Cards are put into pockets. Everyone begins walking around making eye contact with everyone else. The Killer discreetly and secretly winks once in a while at another player. The player must fall forward after he/she takes 10 steps and lets out a yell in agony. The Killer goes about his/her business. A player walking around can yell, "I accuse!" He/she must have another player yell, "I second that." The first accuser says, "I think that it is John." If John is the killer, that round is over. If they are wrong, they die. Continue.

PRUI

Players close their eyes or are blindfolded to begin the game. They begin milling around. When they bump into someone, they shake hands and ask, "Prui?" If the other person asks back, "Prui," they have not yet found the Prui. Find another person to ask. One person has been secretly designated as the Prui. The Prui has eyes open. When someone asks him/her "Prui," there is no response, ask again. If there is no response, you have found the Prui. Now, you're a part of the Prui. Clasp hands with the Prui. When someone bumps you, don't respond. The new members must join your open hand. Keep going until the whole class is connected. Blindfolds optional.

SKIN THE SNAKE

DIRECTIONS:

1. All line up behind one another, facing in the same direction with legs spread astride, feet 18 to 24 inches apart.
2. All bend forward and reach back between the knees with right hand, grasping the left hand of the person behind. At the same time, reach forward with the left hand and grasp the right hand of the person in front.
3. When the line is thus linked, the last person in line crawls between the legs of the next person in front and continues through the entire line, keeping hold of the right hand of the person who was immediately ahead.
4. The next to the last person follows the first crawler, and the entire line follows in order without breaking handholds.
5. Each crawler stands with legs astride when he reaches the head of the line.
6. The stunt ends when the position of the entire line has been reversed.
7. This stunt, done in reverse, is called "Skin the Snake Backwards."

FIND YOUR MATE

Players are given cards with the names of animals, in-
sects, or whatever. Two players have the same animal.
On "Go," players begin making gyrations relating to that
animal. Sooner or later everyone should be paired up and
tell the class what they are. Participants can then show
off their gyrations.

KNOTS

Eight, 10, 12 players form a circle. They take hands with
two other people that are not next to them. (There are
enough hands to work it out). When everyone has 2 hands,
not next to them, they hang on and begin turning their
bodies and unraveling until they are all untangled and
are back in a circle holding hands. Some people will be
facing in; some will be facing out. The activity always
works best with an even number of participants.

THE LAP GAME

Players form a tight circle looking in, shoulder to
shoulder. The referee says, "everyone face to your right."
Everyone makes a ¼ turn. Then they adjust and move in one
step. On command, everyone sits on the person behind them.
If this spectacular group effort works, everyone will be
sitting on everyone's knees. If it flops, everyone will
fall. Try again. When successful, move arms, etc.

GROUP JUGGLING

Players form circles of about 10. One player begins by
throwing an object around such as a ball or frisbee. The
pattern is established as to whom the object is thrown
each time. A new object is worked in, then another, until as many as 4 or 5 objects are flying in pattern form.
If an object is dropped or missed, whoever picks it up
just puts it back into his/her pattern. Use Wiffle balls,
Red balls, Frisbees, Socker balls, whatever.

SNAKE IN THE GRASS

Boundaries are set. The starter snake lies down on the
grass on his/her stomach. Everybody else gathers fear-
lessly around to touch him (one finger will suffice).
When the referee shouts, "Snake in the Grass," everyone
runs within bounds of the snake area. While the snake,
moving on his belly, tries to tag as many as he can.
Those touched become snakes too. Take off your shoes for
more fun. The snakes' hissing always adds excitement.
The last player to be tagged becomes the new snake in the
next game.

HAGOO

Hagoo means, "come here." Teams are lined up facing
each other. One player from each team is selected to go
to the end and begin walking down the center. The object
of the game is for one team to do anything to make the
opposing player break the straight face and smile or
laugh. Any antics are all right except touching. Continue rotating in new players.

Rainy Day Games

KING OR QUEEN UP

EQUIPMENT: 30 - 3 x 5 Cards numbered 1 - 30
Have students place numbered cards on desk tops. One person is selected to be king or queen. The king calls out 6. Six must immediately call out another number such as 8 or call king. Any hesitation and 6 goes to the end of the line and everyone from 6 back moves up one space. The object of the game is to get the king out so that number 1 can take his/her place. Then the king becomes number 30 and everyone moves up one space.
VARIATIONS: Number called cannot call the number previously called before his/hers. Change names of some of the numbers.

CHALKBOARD RELAY

EQUIPMENT: Chalkboard and Chalk
Children are seated in rows facing the chalkboard. The child in the first seat, the Captain, is given a piece of chalk. At a signal, the Captain walks to the board and writes the first word of any sentence. The Captain quickly returns to his/her row and gives the chalk to the second player, who goes to the board and adds the second word to the sentence. As the game progresses, each player within the row adds a word but avoids completing the sentence. It is the duty of the last player in the row to complete the sentence with one word. The first team that completes a sentence in the manner described, is the winner.
TEACHER SUGGESTIONS: While children are gaining experience with this game, it is suggested that the last player in line be allowed any number of words to complete the sentence, instead of only one.
VARIATIONS: Use the same rules to form words from letters. Use the same rules, everyone draws one line until a described picture is complete. Example: Best looking bear.

SIX OBJECT REVERSE PASS LINE RELAY

EQUIPMENT: Six Objects - Bean Bags, Balls, Erasers, Etc. for each group
Players stand in columns facing the front of the room. The first person in each column is the leader. Each leader is provided with six objects. On a given signal, the objects are passed, one at a time, over the left shoulder to the second player. Player #2 must have all six objects in his/her hands before he/she, in turn, passes them to player #3. When the last player in the line has received the six objects, the player calls, "Turn," and all players in the line face the opposite direction. The bean bags are now passed back in the same manner that they were passed forward. The team wins that returns the six objects to the original leader first. The activity can take place with 3, 4, or 5 objects depending on the class.

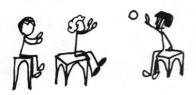

SILENT DYNAMITE

Players sit on desk tops. Three fluff balls are tossed around the room (good tosses, good catches). Players toss balls to players who are looking at them - continuous tossing and catching. When a player misses the ball, or makes a bad toss, he/she sits down. When 10 players or so are sitting down, start over. No talking. If a player makes any noise, he/she sits down also.

WHO'S MISSING

One player leaves the room. The teacher selects one of the room players to hide in the closet. Everyone changes sides. The outside player comes in to the room and is given 30 seconds to guess who is missing. If the correct guess is made within 30 seconds, the guesser gets to choose the next player.

GETTING WARMER

One player leaves the room. The teacher selects one person to put a small object in his/her desk. The class begins clapping moderately. The outside person enters the room and quickly begins moving around the room. As he/she gets closer to the object, the clapping gets louder - softer as the player moves away. The player is given one minute to locate the object. A new player is selected.

COOPERATIVE THREE OBJECT RELAY

The relay is played by children seated in rows. Two rows constitute a team. Players on one team sit facing each other with their feet in a common aisle. Each team has 3 objects placed on the starter's desk. On "Go," the starter hands the first object to the player directly across the row; that player hands it to the next player across the aisle, and the object moves in zig zag fashion down the aisle and back. The second object is started just as soon as the first player can play it. When all objects have gone down and back, the relay is over.
NOTE: Start with just one object, then add a second as understanding increases.

CHARADES

Groups are selected and allowed sufficient time to work out a charade together. A captain is chosen for each group. The word, title, or object chosen by a group should have syllables to make it easier to act out. In deciding upon the method to be used in acting out the ideas, the players remember that all dramatizations are to be in pantomime. Each group has an opportunity to act out its word, name, or title in front of the class. The Captain calls on the class members to guess the syllable or complete word. If the word has not been guessed within a certain time, the Captain tells the class, and the next group prepares to perform. To make the game more interesting, all groups may be asked to decide on a certain general category from which all words must be chosen - famous names, songs, books inventions, cities, countries.

NONELIMINATION SIMON SAYS

The entire class participates in 2, 3, or 4 games, which start at the same time, each with a leader who performs various movements by saying, "Simon says," and the children are to imitate the movement. If the leader neglects to say "Simon says," the child is transferred to one of the other games. This way, no one is eliminated from the game.

FOOTBALL UPSET

All players are seated except for the leader. All players have been designated to be one of five positions on a football team - quarterback, wide receivers, fullbacks, centers, tight ends. Positions are evenly distributed. The leader, who also has a position for the game, calls out, "Fullbacks." All fullbacks attempt to change seats with each other while the leader attempts to sit in a seat. One fullback is left out; he/she calls a new position, and the game continues.
NOTE: Student can sit on desk tops.

SEVEN UP

Seven children are chosen to stand side by side in front of the room. The appointed leader of this group gives the command, "Heads down - Thumbs up!" On this command, the seated children close their eyes, lower their heads, and leave one thumb extended in the air. At this time, each of the seven players quietly circulates among the tables or desks and touches one of the seated children on the thumb. Each child returns to his/her original position in front of the room. When all 7 players return to the front of the room, the leader says, "Heads up, Seven up!" On this command, all children raise their heads, and the 7 tagged children try and guess who it was that tagged them. If they guess correctly, he/she takes the place at the front of the room, and the player that tagged him/her sits down and participates.

SIX OBJECT BASKET RELAY

EQUIPMENT: Bean Bag or Eraser
Children are seated in rows. Each row constitutes one team. All rows must have the same number of players. The first player in each row is the Captain. On his/her desk are the same number of objects as there are players in the row (Captain included). A container - basket, box, circle drawn on the floor, etc. - is placed in front of each Captain. On a given signal, each Captain picks up one object and passes it over his/her left shoulder to player #2, who passes it to player #3, and so on. This action is repeated by each player on every team. When the last player in the row receives the object, he/she leaves his/her seat, walks swiftly, but safely, to the front of the row and deposits the objects in the basket. At this time, all players in the row rise and move back one seat. This action leaves the front seat vacant for the player who put the objects in the basket. When this player is seated, he/she picks up another object from the top of the desk and passes it back as before.
NOTE: Have players and Captains use the same side to make the switches.
VARIATION: Use one eraser per row. Have the last player bring the eraser to the front desk, sit down, and pass it back when everyone is back in position. The relay is over.

PASS 'N DUCK CLASSROOM RELAYS

Players stand in lines beside their desks with the Captain standing about 5' away facing toward the relay team. The Captain passes the ball to #1 player. #1 player passes it back to the Captain and ducks. The Captain passes the ball to #2 player; #2 player passes the ball back and ducks. This continues until the last player passes back to the Captain, ducks; and the Captain ducks and yells, "Done." The first team to finish wins the round. Pick new Captain; continue.

RING ON A STRING

EQUIPMENT: One large String, 15' approximately, tied together at ends with ring attached. Circles of 10 players a
formed with 1 player standing in the middle. The string wi
the ring is held loosely in both hands by all players in th
seated circle. The object of the game is to slip the ring
along the string from one player to the next while "It" tri
to locate the ring or who has it. The player who is successful, changes places with the one under whose hand the
ring was. If unsuccessful, he/she continues as "It."

WHO CHANGED THE MOTION?

The whole class plays. Players sit in a circle. One playe
is "It" and leaves the room. Another player is selected to
be a leader and starts a motion (swings arms, taps head,
wiggles foot, etc.) which the other players immediately fol
low. "It" is called back into the room, and the group follows the leader, changing from motion to motion. "It,"
standing in the center of the circle, tries to guess who is
the leader, and players try to confuse "It" by looking at
each other as they follow the changes. The leader also tri
to confuse "It" by looking at another player as though that
player was the leader.

DICTIONARY "HIDE-IT"

The whole class plays in rows, with a dictionary and one
eraser for each row. One person, from each row, comes forward and stands in front of his/her row, facing the front c
the room. As the leader reads words from the dictionary, a
a fairly rapid rate, the players in each row quickly pass t
eraser up and down from one person to the next. As soon a
the leader stops reading, the person with the eraser quick
hides it. At the same time, the person standing at the fr
of the row whirls around to identify who has the eraser before he/she can hide it. If the player at the front of th
row identifies the person with the eraser, they change pla
and the game continues. Suggestion - teacher can also use
record instead of the dictionary.

DO THIS, DO THAT

One child is the leader and performs various movements whi
are accompanied by either "Do This" or "Do That." All pla
ers must execute the movements which are accompanied by "D
This." If the directions are "Do That," no one is to move
Those who move at the wrong time are eliminated and sit do
in place. (Take off on Simon Says). Show child movements
performed by any part of the body to music. Class will ne
help in building up their vocabulary of body parts.

STATUE

Children mimic animals, merry-go-round, airplane, etc. Wh
music stops, everyone freezes in the same position. Teach
brings attention of everyone to the "funniest" statue.

BELLRINGER

One person is chosen to leave the room. Players stand sho
der to shoulder, in a row, with their hands behind their
backs. One player is given a bell. When the person chose
to leave returns, the player with the bell rings it once.
The person then decides who rang the bell. If the person
guesses right, he/she gets another turn. If not, the one
with the bell gets to leave the room. Have 3 teams; only
or 3 guesses.

BALLOON BALL

The class is divided into two teams. Rows 1, 3, and 5 are
Team A. Rows 2, 4, and 6 are Team B. The aisle near the
windows is Team A's goal, and the aisle near the side wall
is Team B's goal; or the left and right sides of the room
may be the goals. Three balloons are tossed into the air in
the center of the room by the teacher. The seated players
strike them with the open hand and try to get it over their
opponent's goal. Players may not strike the balloons with
their fists or leave their seats. If either of these violations is committed, the balloon is tossed into the air by a
member of the team that committed the violation. Each goal
counts one point. The team scoring the greater number of
points wins the game. If too many goals are made, one player from each team may be chosen to be goalkeeper. They may
stand and try to prevent the balloons from striking the
floor in their respective goal areas.

BALLOON VOLLEYBALL

EQUIPMENT: 5 Balloons
FORMATION: Yarn across the middle of the classroom
PLAYERS: Whole Class
This is an informal game with children trying to bat the
ball back and forth across the rope. Two balloons should be
used for variation. If children are sitting on the floor,
put yarn 3' from floor; if children are at their seats, put
yarn 5' high. Scoring is done when side fails to control a
ball and allows it to touch the floor or wall. The balloon
can be batted as often as possible.
VARIATION: If a marble or button is put inside the balloon,
the balloon will take an erratic pat adding interest to the
game. Could be 2 against 2 or more.

KEEP THE BALLOON UP FOR TIME

All players are seated - players must remain seated the
entire time. (No raising of the bottoms off of the seat.)
The teacher passes out 10, 11, 12, 13, 14, 15 balloons.
Students top them up at the same time. The class keeps all
of the balloons topped up as long as possible. Set a new
record for elapsed time. Break the record - move from this
activity to classroom balloon volleyball.
NOTE: Begin with a few balloons.

TIME BOMB

The entire class uses erasers or similar objects. Someone
is chosen to leave the class while another person in the
class puts the eraser in plain sight. The person outside is
called back into the room to look for it. The class counts
aloud while the person looks for the object. As he/she
gets closer, the class counts louder; and, as he/she gets
farther away, the class counts softer. Suggestions: Have
the person who finds the eraser choose another person to
go out. Have the class determine what number they are
going to count to before time is up and the time bomb
explodes.

INDIVIDUAL RAINY DAY AND SPARE TIME TABLE TOP ACTIVITIES

THE 19 PIECE PUZZLE - SIX 2" x 2" SQUARES

Cut out 6 pieces of posterboard 2" x 2". Then, cut the
2" x 2" squares into pieces as seen on diagram. Place
them in an envelope with directions on the outside:
Put this puzzle together, make six 2" x 2" squares.

ENCODING ACTIVITY

Take any random six consonants and the five vowels
doubled. Print them on pieces of tagboard. Spread them
out on your desk and see how many words that you can make
in 10 minutes. Points: 2 for 2-letter words; 3 for 3-
letter words, etc. Mix all letters back into the pile
after each word is developed. List the words on a piece
of paper. Note to Teachers: Make several sets of enve-
lopes with different consonants. Have them on hand for
rainy day and spare time activities.

3/4" x 3/4" Tagboard Squares:

B K J T S L A E I O U A
E I O U

DRAW THE OTHER HALF

Find a magazine with some great picture inside. Cut out a picture of a face, ear, or something that interests you. Now, cut the picture in half vertically. Paste half of the picture on a piece of ditto paper and see if you can draw the other half of the picture without looking at it.
VARIATION: Distort the picture. Draw the other half of a car - make it much longer or much shorter than actual size.

EXPAND A PICTURE

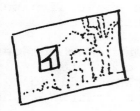

Find another interesting picture in a magazine. Cut out a 2" x 2" square of some part of that picture. Now, paste the 2" x 2" square on a piece of ditto paper and create an interesting picture while using the square as a beginning for your creation.

ENLARGE A PICTURE

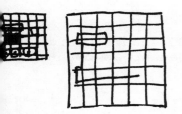

Find a small picture that you like in a magazine. Draw ¼" lines both vertically and horizontally across the small picture. Now, draw 1" lines both vertically and horizontally on a piece of ditto paper. Match the lines and spaces and draw just what you see in a square on the small picture on one square of the larger grid. Result: A copy of the smaller picture enlarged. (Four times larger than before.)

RHYTHM STICK PASSING PRACTICE

Players sit on the floor with legs crossed and are facing each other. Each player is holding two rhythm sticks. Players exchange sticks by tossing sticks that are held in the same hands. Right hand toss - right catch (exchange). In between exchanges, players create taps and stick flips simultaneously.
NOTE: Toss sticks toward partner's chest, not towards hand.

CHIP FLIP AND CATCH PARTNER CHALLENGE

Several 1" x 1" posterboard chips should be available to players. The first player sets 2 chips on the back of his forearms, near the elbow, which is bent backward and is parallel with the ground. He/she then straightens arm and catches the chips in mid air with the hand. The partner must then repeat this trick. If the partner is successful, he/she then adds a couple of chips and repeats the trick and challenges. How many chips can you catch?
NOTE: Use pennies or plastic chips also. Try the trick with your other hand.

TABLE TOP CARD SORTING

Use a stop watch and a deck of playing cards. One player times and the other sorts. The task is to separate the cards into 2 piles.

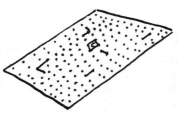

TASK	TIME
1. Red and Black (face up)	1. _____
2. Red and Black (face down)	2. _____
3. Suits (face up)	3. _____
4. Suits (face down)	4. _____
5. By Number (1, 2, 3...face up)	5. _____
6. By Number (face down)	6. _____
7. 7 & below, 8 & above (face up)	7. _____
8. 7 & below, 8 & above (face down)	8. _____

MAKE SQUARES

Two players use pencil and paper. Prepare a sheet of paper for each pair of players with 5 or more vertical rows of dots. Players take turns connecting any 2 dots with a straight line. No diagonal line may be drawn. Each places his/her initial in each square his/her line completes. Each completed square rates an extra turn. When all dots are connected, player with the most completed squares, wins.

GO (TWO PLAYERS)

The object of GO is to get five markers in a row, horizontally, vertically, or diagonally, and be the first of the two players to do so. Play on the 100 square board and use two different sets of markers. Set up an open-ended situation.

SIX TO MAKE FOUR (TWO PLAYERS)

Play on a 36 square board (6 squares x 6 squares). Players play a total of 6 markers each. The object of the game is to be the first player to get 4 in a row horizontally, vertically, or diagonally. When the 12 markers are down and no one has 4 in a row, the player who took the first turn can move one marker and slide one space or jump over another marker (either his/her own or his/her opponent's) to continue to try to get 4 in a row.

TIC TAC TOE (TWO PLAYERS)

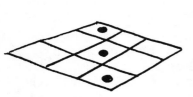

Play on a 3 x 3 square board (2½" squares). The object of the game is to get 3 in a row horizontally, vertically, or diagonally. Players play a total of 3 markers each. When all 6 markers are down and no one has 3 in a row, the player who took the first turn can move one marker and either slide one space or jump over another marker (his/her own or his/her opponent's) to continue to try to get 3 in a row. Take turns.

JACKS FOR TWO

Using Jacks and ball, players play regular rules for Jacks - pick up the ones, two, etc. Players can also play "Can You Challenge?" Jacks and make up challenges for each other.

PICK UP STICKS FOR TWO

Use a set of pick up sticks. Players play regular or classroom rules for pick up sticks - a floor activity.

TOSS THE CARDS IN THE CAN

Use 2 decks of cards, a #10 can, from the cook, and 2
chairs. Players sit on chairs backwards with the can set
an equal distance between them. Each player is holding a
deck of cards. On the signal, they both begin attempting
to toss the cards one at a time over the back of their
chairs into the can. The player with the most cards tossed
into the can, wins.

TRIANGLE FOOTBALL

Players can play on the table, desk top, or the floor if
lines are drawn or used. The object of the game is to make
the triangle bend so that it is hanging over the edge of the
table top, desk top, or line. Each player gets 3 downs or
3 flicks with a finger to move the triangle across the sur-
face and make it land on the edge. If successful, 6 points
are alloted; the football is brought back to the scoring
player's 20 yard line and stood on end with the flat side
facing him/her. He/she then flicks the object with the
middle finger while the opposing player holds hands in
goal post position. The scoring player attempts to flick
the triangle through the goal post upright for the extra
point. The triangle is turned over to the opposing player.
NOTE: If the triangle goes off of the edge of the table on
any down, it is customarily turned over to opposing player.

CLOTHES PIN DROP

Use clothes pins and tennis ball cans. Each player has a
specified number of clothes pins to drop in his/her tennis
ball can. Players stand and hold the pins up to their chins
and aim, release the clothes pins, and hope that they fall
directly into the can. The player with the most pins in the
can wins that round.

POOR MAN'S AIR HOCKEY

Hockey equipment: 6 poker chips glued together to make 2
hammers and a puck. Each player presses fingers down on the
chip (hammer). One chip is in the center and becomes the
puck. The object of the game is to hit the puck hard so
that it goes off the other side of the table. Hammers are
never released to hit the puck. NOTE: Books are lined up on
each side to make an alley way and walls to keep puck in
bounds. Go for it!

RHYTHM STICK HOCKEY

Use 2 rhythm sticks and a tennis ball. Each player uses his/
her rhythm stick as a Hockey stick. Players sit on floor
with legs apart. Legs serve as goals. Players tap the ball
back and forth, attempting to make a goal. Goal: If the
ball touches the opposing player above the knee (thigh area),
a goal is scored. If the ball is hit outside of feet, a goal
is scored. Set the distance - rapid play.
VARIATION: Sit a lot farther apart. Use a styrofoam cup
for a target in the middle.

BEAN BAG GRAB

Sit down on floor or chair and place a bean bag between you.
Place hands on hips. One player says, "right," "left," or
"both hands;" and both reach for bean bag. Play 10 seconds.

HAND BASEBALL

Two players. A decision is made as to who bats first. The
two children may sit or stand to play. Each player puts one
hand behind his/her back. On a signal, each player sticks
out his/her hand with one to five fingers showing. Totals
are then made for both players. Even numbers help the batte
while odd numbers help the pitcher. All runners must be
forced to the next base. Runners may not advance on an out.
On a double play, the batter plus the runner on the nearest
base to home is out. A double or triple play with the bases
empty means only one out. A triple play with one person on
base means two outs.

CODE

EVEN	ODD
2 fingers - walk	3 fingers - out
4 fingers - single	5 fingers - out
6 fingers - double	7 fingers - double play
8 fingers - triple	9 fingers - triple play
10 fingers - homerun	

WAR

Addition or multiplication (decide). Each player holds a
deck of cards face down in his/her hand. The deck consists
of 15 numbered cards. 0, 1, 2, 3, 4, 5, 6, 7, 8, 9, 5, 6,
7, 8, 9. Decks are made from 2 different colors of poster
board. Red deck/yellow deck, etc. Both players turn cards
over at the same time and respond to the cards by adding or
multiplying. The player who responds first, takes both
cards. The winner is the player with the most cards at the
end of the game.
VARIATION: If 2 cards are turned up that are the same (8
and 8, for example), play the next card face down on top of
the 8's. Play the next card face up for all cards in the
center of the table.

HANGMAN

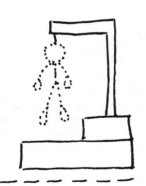

Play on the other side of a used ditto. One player draws a
guillotine. Next, the player thinks of a word and draws a
short line for each letter in the word under the guillotine.
The other player attempts to guess the word by guessing one
letter at a time. If the letter fits into the word, the
guillotine player records it on one of the short lines in
the correct place. If the letter does not fit, the guillotine player writes it on the paper and draws one part of
the man to be hung. (Head, neck, torso, arms, legs, hands,
feet). The object is to guess the word before the man is
hung. The guesser can guess the whole word at any time; but
if wrong, another body part is drawn.

CHAIR RING TOSS - JUST OUTSIDE THE DOOR

Turn a chair over and use the rungs for targets; each rung
has a certain value. Players set distance and make the rule

TABLE TOP ARM WRESTLING AND THUMB WRESTLING

Arm Wrestling: Each player places elbow on the table and
grasps hands with opponent - right hand/right hand. On "Go,
players attempt to push opponent's arm down and make it touc
the table. NOTE: Try your other arm.
Thumb Wrestling: Grip right hand to right hand (or left to
left), pressing thumbs together. On signal, separate thumbs
and try to pin opponent's thumb for a 3 count.

RAINY DAY ACTIVITIES FOR 6

HUMAN TIC TAC TOE
Use three X sheets, 8 x 10, and three O sheets, 8 x 10, with strings attached so that they hang in front of the players. Teams of three put on tagboard Xs and Os. Nine mats or squares are laid out on the floor. One team goes first, a player places himself/herself on a mat; the next team goes, etc. When all six players are on the mats and there is not a tic tac toe, the first team can move one player. Then the other team can move one player until one team out-maneuvers the other team.

HUMAN SWITCH
Use three Xs and three Os, 8 x 10 sheets with string to hang around players' necks and hang in front; mats or squares to stand on, 7 per group of 6 players. The object of the game is to have the three Xs change places with the three Os in the fewest amount of moves possible. Players are allowed to step sideways one place or jump over one player. Players must move one at a time. This is a team effort with team decision making. (15 moves).

MEMORY CARDS
Several direction cards are made by the teacher or class. Continuous directions from 2 to .... The card may say, "Go over to the pencil sharpener, touch it, walk left 3 steps, spin around once, look out the window, walk back to your seat." The student is given a few seconds to lock it in. Then he gives the card to someone and attempts to do what is stated on the card. Cards can be increased or decreased in difficulty.

CIRCLE RHYTHM CLAPPING
Players form a circle with number cards placed in order on the floor - 1, 2, 3, 4, 5, 6 - one in front of each player. The object of the game is to get to be the #1 player and stay there. Someone starts - two knee slaps, two hand claps, snap left hand (thumb and middle finger), snap right hand (thumb and middle finger). The starting player says his/her own number on the first snap. Example: 6 and a new number on the second snap (4). Then everyone starts again: slap, slap, clap, clap, and #4 says 4 on first finger snap and a new number on second snap. Continue. If a player misses, he/she moves to card #6, and everyone moves up one card that can move.

WHO CHANGED THE DIRECTION ARROW, SHAPE,
NUMBER, COLOR, DICE, PATTERN, LETTER, ETC.
Need 6 players, 18 - 9 x 12 cards with a theme. (Example: shapes). One student stands facing away from a line of 5 or 6 students. On "Go," he spins around and glances at students holding cards with various shapes. He locks it in, spins away. One person changes their shape card or moves it ¼ turn. Each student would be holding 3 cards, one behind the other. The student facing away spins around again and attempts to select the player who changed cards. If successful, he/she takes his/her place. Each time he/she misses, he/she adds a point to the score. Only one guess per time. Continuous play.

Quick Hands

How many switches can you make in 30 seconds?

Hold the ball between your knees, one hand in front, one hand around a leg - Do not let the ball touch your knees. Switch hands 6 times without missing.

Limbo

Wand Balance Catch

Balance the wand on your fingers or palm. Flip the wand upward, let it turn end-to-end once. Catch it by balancing it on your fingers or palm.

Chair Dips for Time

Put your feet out in front. Push yourself up, let yourself down. How many can you do in 30 seconds? How long can you stay suspended with only your hands for support on the chairs?

Small Space Contests

Rainy Day Classroom

Wand Elbow Balance

Balance the wand on your elbow for 5 seconds. Try for 6-10 seconds.

Paper Bag Jump for Time

How many jumps can you do in 15 seconds?

Stand beside your paper bag, jump over the bag sideways, back and forth. Use the same size bag everytime.

Elbow Coin Flip

Flick the cards into the can. Record hits.

Jump Rope
How many consecutive jumps in 10 seconds?

Hula Hooping for Time
How long can you keep it up?

Hoop Sloop for Time
Two minutes. Put your body through the hoop. How many times can you put your body through the hoop in two minutes?

Juggle two balls with one hand. How many times? How many times in one minute?

Head Tilt
Bean bag catch between knees. How many catches in 3 minutes?

Beach Ball Juggling. How many consecutive juggles can you make? Knee, foot, head.

Dribble City
Dribble the ball all the way around your body. How many times can you dribble around in one minute?

Loco Ball
Tap it up, keep it going, either hand.

Slip the Hoop
Use only your feet to get out. Elasped time!

Step Through for Time
How many step throughs can you make in 30 seconds? Hold your wand overhead. On "Go" step through the wand, one foot then the other. Step back through the other way. Count each forward and backward step through.

Side Paddle Taps

Flat   side

Begin by tapping the ball up on the flat part of the paddle. When you are ready, tap the ball up once on the side of the paddle. Recover with flat paddle taps, tap on side, recover, side ... Continuous tapping. Select the best level or standard for you. 5-8-10 side paddle taps completes the challenge.

Jacks Contest
1. Pick up jacks for time.
2. Ones, twos ... How far can you go?
3. Put dots on the floor for jack-spaces.

Football Leadup Games and Activities

TOUCHDOWN

Players are designated to each end of the field - one team has pinnies on, both teams have flags in their back pockets. Teams huddle and decide who holds the beans; five beans are handed out. Each player closes his/her fists as if he/she were holding the beans. The Bean Team yells, "Here we come." The object is for the person holding the object to make it across the opposing team's goal line without getting his/her flag pulled. The teams should end at the opposite ends of the field. Each team gets 2 turns, then the other team gets 2 turns. One point is given for a touchdown.
NOTES: Many Chasing-Fleeing games fit into format - just change number of players. Opposing team attempts to pull everyone's flag in pursuit of people carrying objects.

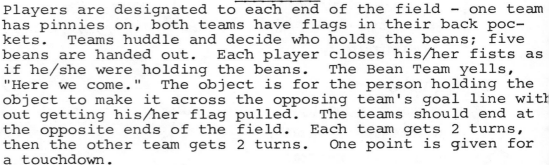

HIGH TOSS FOOTBALL

Players on both teams stand around the tosser or person holding the ball. Each player has on a flag; one team has pinnies. The tosser tosses the ball straight up in the air. Players on both teams attempt to catch the ball. When a player from one team catches the ball, he/she runs toward the goal. When his/her flag is pulled, he/she stops, puts flag back in and tosses the ball straight up for a new play. The tosser cannot catch the ball. One point is scored for each touchdown. Go back to center of field and high toss football.
NOTE: Keep 2 balls going with 30 players. (It works out).

SPEEDBALL/FOOTBALL

Players are divided into 2 equal teams. All players have on football flags. One team begins with the ball about 1/3 of the way up the field. The objective is to get the ball across your opponent's goal line by running or passing the ball without (1) letting the ball drop to the ground, (2) getting your flag pulled when you have the ball, (3) getting intercepted. All three items result in a turnover, and the ball goes to the other team on the spot. Teams must pass to at least three people before they can cross their opponent's goal line. If a team intercepts on the one foot line, the ball must be passed to three people (minimum) before a touchdown can be made.
VARIATIONS: Run 2 games at the same time. Use short fields for success and motivation. Play this game with frisbees.

SACK THE QUARTERBACK

Two players are selected to be sackers. The rest of the
players are quarterbacks. The job of the sacker is to encourage quarterbacks to come as close or into the circle, if
possible; then at a split second, yell, "Sack." The quarterbacks take off and attempt to get across the line before
their flag is pulled. If their flag is pulled before they
cross the line, they become sackers and help out the other
sackers.
NOTE: Variation to increase intensity and skill - have each
quarterback come into the court bouncing or throwing up a
7" ball, or some object. When the signal to run is yelled,
the quarterbacks retrieve their balls and run.

KICK OFF KICKBALL/PASS IT AROUND

Teams are equal; one team is up to kick as in kickball. Two
footballs are T'd up next to home plate. The kicker runs up,
eye on ball, kicks off into field of play. The kicker then
attempts to run the bases for a home run before someone in
the field catches or picks up the football and passes it to
a close player. The ball must be passed from one player to
another until everyone has touched it. If the runner circles the bases before everyone has received the ball, he/she
scores one run for the team. If the team in field finishes
the passes to everyone, the runner is out.
NOTES: Players in field cannot move closer, once the ball
is caught by the first player. Adjust bases in and out
until you have the distance correct. Let everyone on the
up team kick before you change sides. Count the runs, not
the outs.

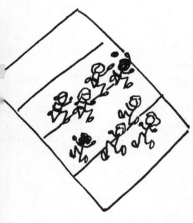

FIRST DOWN FLAG FOOTBALL
(For More Success on Offense)

The object of this game is to keep the players moving and
thinking about strategy and success.
First Down Number One Rule:
The field is set up and marked off in quarters. The offensive team receives a first down each time that they cross
over a quarter of the field line with the ball.
First Down Number Two Rule:
The offensive team receives a first down each time that it
completes 3 passes in 4 downs.

Regular flag football rules apply except for first downs.
NOTE: Play this game with a tennis ball! Action!

FIVE HUNDRED

The up player punts the soccer balls into the field. Field
players score a certain number of points, depending on how
they receive the ball.

    a. Caught on fly 100
    b. Caught on first bounce 75
    c. Caught on second bounce 50
    d. Missed 0

Players continue to add cumulative points. First player
to go over 500 becomes the next punter.

NEWCOMB WITH A FOOTBALL

Teams of 7 or 8 are placed on each half of the court. The
ball is put in play by a player in the back line throwing
the ball over the net. Each team must have "3" players
handle the ball before it returns over the net. The 3rd
person returns the ball. Have the players handle the ball
like a hot potato for fast action. No reaching over the
net - a chalk line about 2" from net stops this. If a
ball is dropped or lands in bounds, a hesitation is called,
or repeat players handle the ball 1-2-1. A point is
scored if the winning side served. Otherwise, the serving
team loses its serve.
VARIATION: (Play Deck Tennis) with deck rings - underhand
toss. (Catch up Ball-Low Net) start a ball from each side
of net at the same time. If both balls are in possession
on the same side, the other team receives a point - fast
action.

TEN CATCHES - KEEP AWAY
(Passing, Receiving Agility)

An area or field is coned off for play. One team has on
pinnies, and both teams have on flags. A player from X
begins play by passing to a teammate. The object of the
game is to pass 10 consecutive times to teammates without:
(1) dropping a pass, (2) fumbling, (3) getting intercepted,
and (4) getting your flag pulled when you have the ball.
Any infractions result in a turnover, and the other team
starts. If 10 straight catches are made, 6 points are
awarded, and the other team starts. No one can pull the
starting player's flag.
NOTES: Begin with 5 completions; as players become better,
move to 6, 7, etc. This is an extremely active game; 10 -
15 minutes should be enough for one P.E. period before you
move students to another activity.

PUNT, PASS, OR KICK SCHOOL OR CLASS CONTEST

EQUIPMENT: A straight line about 120' marked off in 10'
lengths, measuring tape, markers for where ball lands, scor
sheet, lots of help from students.
Whether punting, passing or place kicking is taking place,
the actual distance that the ball travels on the fly from
the starting line until it hits the ground is measured. An
adjustment is made for distance away from the line.
EXAMPLE: If the ball is thrown 50' and lands 5' off of the
line, the distance awarded is 45'; 45 points would be what
the participant received if that was the best thrown. Add
those points to the punt and place kicking points for a
grand total.

PUNT BACK
(Punting, Judging Distance, Catching)

Players take the field as teams. One team punts the ball
to the other team. A team player catches the ball or stops
the ball, picks it up, and punts it away to the other team
from the point of control. Eventually, one team will punt
the ball deep enough to cross the back goal line. One poin
is awarded for punting the ball across the line. Play is
started again from 1/2 the distance to the center.
NOTE: Adjust field sizes with cones.

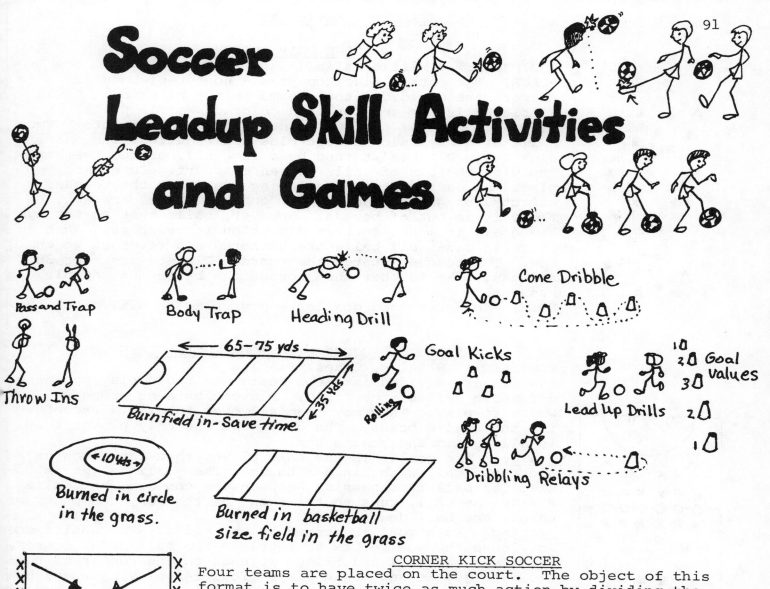

Soccer Leadup Skill Activities and Games

Pass and Trap

Body Trap

Heading Drill

Cone Dribble

Throw Ins

65-75 yds

35 yds

Burn field in - Save time

Rolling

Goal Kicks

Lead Up Drills

1☐
2☐ Goal
3☐ Values

2☐

1☐

Dribbling Relays

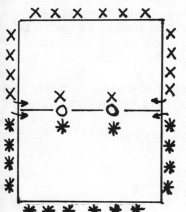

←10 yds→

Burned in circle in the grass.

Burned in basketball size field in the grass

CORNER KICK SOCCER

Four teams are placed on the court. The object of this format is to have twice as much action by dividing the court into 2 games. When the teacher blows the whistle, all 8 corner players come out and attempt to kick the ball across the opponent's goal line. The players on the line use their feet to keep the ball from coming across the line. Everyone is involved. When the goals are scored, the court players return to center and get back in center of line. Corner players resume new play on the whistle. Set a time limit for scoring.
NOTE: Skills can be added. One pass, two passes, before scoring, etc.

LINE SOCCER

Teams of 14-15 are placed around the court. The 4 players nearest ½ court enter the court. The players in the end zone are goalies and may stop the ball with any part of their bodies except hands and arms. The side line players keep the ball kicked in bounds and in play. After a goal is kicked at either end, the court players return directly to the center of their end zone and two new players from each team enter the court. Resume play by putting ball in center, facing off and blowing whistle.
VARIATION: Two passes before scoring etc.; each player puts foot on the ball to start.

BLUE CHIP SOCCER

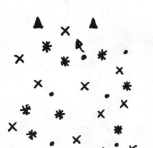

EQUIPMENT: 7 Wiffle Balls
PLACE: The entire Blacktop Area - no out-of-bounds.
Players are divided into 2 teams on the blacktop. Seven
Wiffle Balls are set for each color of Wiffle Balls.
Blue - 10 points; red - 6 points; yellow - 2 points. Two
balls of every color except blue are required; use one
blue ball. Play is started by a face off, or the teacher
emptying the box of balls at center court. Cones are
placed at each end of the playing area that the teacher
selects for goals. No side or end boundaries are set.
There is no out of bounds. However, balls must go through
the goals from the correct direction for a score. When a
score is made, all balls are gathered and returned to the
box. The teacher states the score. Players rest for 30
seconds. The teacher then tosses the balls out and play
resumes.
NOTE: No designated goalies - your players will catch on
and handle it!

SIX BALL SOCCER WITH YOUR WHOLE CLASS

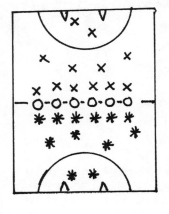

EQUIPMENT: 6 Balls, Cones, Pinnies
Players are divided into two teams and begin play on their
defensive half of the field. Players have no areas in
which to play. They may roam all over the field except
for the goalie boxes. The goalie is the only player that
is allowed in the goalie box.
Goalie: The goalie is the only player that can touch or
pick up a ball with his/her hands. The goalie's job is to
keep the ball from passing between the cones. The goalie
fields the ball, runs to the front of the box, and punts or
throws the ball down field.
Scoring: Each goal is scored as one point. The goalie does
not leave the goalie box to retrieve the ball. The scorer
retrieves the ball and brings it back to the center of their
field to juggle and begin play. To speed play, just have
the goalie punt the ball after a goal.
The game is continuously played. The only ball not in play
is the one being brought back to the center for rejuggling.
Regular elementary soccer skills and rules. Call hands,
fouls, etc.
NOTES: Use 2 goalies - one chases the ball. Out-of-bounds
the other team has a throw-in.

CRAB SOCCER

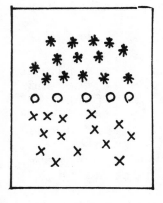

Players are divided into 2 teams and placed on the court in
crab walk position. On the whistle, both teams (in crab
position) attempt to kick the balls across their opponent's
end line for a goal and one point. After a goal is scored,
the teacher tosses the ball back in play for continuous
action. Balls that go outside are tossed back in. In the
M. P. Room, there is no out-of-bounds.
NOTES: Four balls in the game give everyone opportunity to
participate. Every time a ball hits the opposite wall, a
goal is scored.
VARIATION: Play 2 games - 7 or 8 on a side across M. P.
Room.

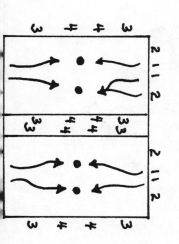

EQUIPMENT: 4 Balls
Teams of 8 are placed on the court with each player aware
of his/her position number - 1, 2, 3, or 4. Balls are
placed on the center line. On the whistle, the number 1's
run out and attempt to maneuver the ball past their opponents and kick it through their goal line and hit the wall.
A goal is scored if the ball passes the line or hits the
M.P. Room wall. The job of the number 2 players is to move
over and play goalie and keep the ball from going through.
The job of the 3rd and 4th players is to stay out of bounds,
use their feet, and keep the ball from going out of bounds.
Blow the whistle to begin play. If a score has not been
made with both balls in one minute, blow the whistle and
stop play. The 4's become 3's - 3's become 2's - 2's
become 1's - 1's become 4's. Resume play. One point is
awarded for each goal.
NOTES: Use small numbered cards on the floor the first day.
Play 2 games cross court in your M.P. Room. Great on the
grass also.

CIRCLE SOCCER

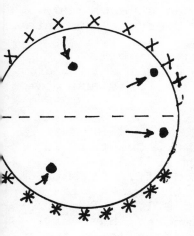

Player takes position as seen in diagram. The object of
the game is to kick a ball past one of your opponents. The
ball must travel out shoulder height or lower to be counted
for a score. One point is accorded for each goal. Players
can block or trap the ball with any part of the body except
hands and arms.
NOTE: Use 4 soccer balls for more action.
VARIATION: Move in and join hands and play.

SIX BALL SOCCER BALL DRIBBLING TAG

EQUIPMENT: 6 Balls, 6 Pinnies
Six players have pinnies on and balls on the ground in front
of them. See diagram. The remainder of the class is scattered in the field. The six players take off dribbling the
ball and attempting to hit scattering players below the
waist with the ball (stay in control). When a scattering
player is hit, he/she becomes a sideline player and stays
out of bounds. The task of the hit players is to work as
sideline helpers and kick the ball at scattering players or
back to dribblers. When the scattering players are down
to six, they change places, put the pinnies on, and everyone
is back in the game.
VARIATION: Tagged players take the ball. Everyone stays
in. Continuous play.

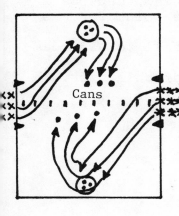

SOCCER WARM UP

EQUIPMENT: 2 Bike Tires, 6 Balls, 6 - 10 Tennis Ball Cans,
4 Cones
Players are divided into 2 teams. Teams line up on boundary
lines facing each other. On signal, 3 players from each team
(the players standing between the cones) run to the bike tire
take a ball and dribble the ball with their feet to the pins,
trying to knock them down. The player who knocks over a pin
first, scores one point for his/her team. When players finish, they rotate to the end of their line.
NOTES: Use of 6 balls and 6 participants each time provides for maximum participation. Set up 10 pins for maximum activity. Tennis ball cans work in place of bowling
pins. Next participants run out and set up pins as last
participants are taking balls back to tires. Fast action.

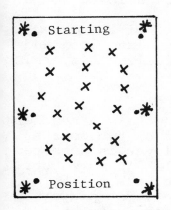

Basketball Leadup Activities

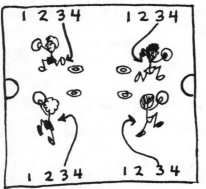

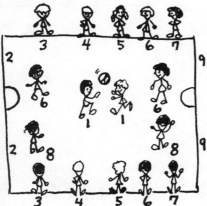

BARREL BALL BASKETBALL

Played with a soccer ball or volleyball - <u>4th grade</u>.
Collect 4 trash cans from behind the kitchen and collect
2 long turning ropes. Set the bottom can upside down, the
top can right side up on top of bottom can at each end.
Rope off an area to stop goal tending. Everyone must stay
out of roped area.
SKILL: To teach students to move without the ball.
"NO DRIBBLING ALLOWED." Each team must pass the ball down
court without taking steps, learn to pivot, pass and move
into open spaces without the ball.

SIDELINE BASKETBALL

Teams of 10 can all be a part of the game. One team is
lined up on one sideline, the other team is lined up on
the other sideline. Players are numbered off. Attempt
to have boys/girls numbers correspond with boys/girls
on other team. Three numbers are called - 1, 6, 8. The
first number called, #1, becomes the jumpers. Numbers 6
and 8 become team members. Two minutes are allowed for a
team to score.
NOTE: The sideline players are also a part of the game.
Team players can pass to sideline, then run into open and
have ball passed back to them. Use the sideline players.

NUMBERS (TEAM) BASKETBALL

EQUIPMENT: 4 Balls, 4 Deck Rings
Players are divided into 4 equal teams. (Note: A teacher
could have 8 equal teams and run this game on two courts
side by side. Total class.) Each team player is numbered
off from 1 - 4. The teacher calls #3. All 3's come out,
take the balls off the deck rings, dribble back to the
basket and attempt to shoot a basket. The first player
to make a basket, dribbles back to deck ring; sets ball
down and runs across the line, scores one point for his/
her team.
VARIATION: Dribble back and chest pass ball to all teammates instead of shooting a basket.
VARIATION: After 3 attempts at basket, dribble back.

FIGURE 8 RELAYS

Six teams of 5 are set up on the court. On "Go," the first player in each line takes off - goes around the cone in front of the line, dribbles around next cone to left - dribbles around cone in front of his/her line, dribbles to mat and passes to next player. Continue. When everyone is back in position, relay is over.
NOTE: Middle lines always go to left. Go over all patterns with all teams. Let them walk through.

BALL FLAG TAG

EQUIPMENT: 30 - 7" Balls, 30 Flags
Concept - nobody out! Keep your eyes up! All players have flags on back pockets or close - same amount of flag showing for each player. Players begin dribbling around attempting to pull everyone else's flags. When a player pulls a flag, he/she dribbles over to the teacher and gives the flag to him/her. The flagless players come to the teacher, get a flag, dribble to wall, slap the wall, and they're back in the game. Fun stuff! Start with one-on-one drills - pulling flags.

BALL HANDLING ACTIVITIES
SOME RELAYS

STRIDE BALL RELAYS

Teams of 5 are lined up. First player passes ball between legs to next player - to next - last player runs forward and starts ball again. Continue. When all players are in starting positions, the relay is over.

PASS OR DUCK RELAYS

Teams of 5 are lined up. The first player steps out 4 or 5 steps, faces team. First player passes the ball to first player in line (chest passes). Player passes ball back, ducks; first player passes to second player. Same procedure. First player ducks when ball is received for last time.

OVER 'N OVER RELAYS - TOTAL MOVEMENT EDUCATION RELAY

Teams of 5 are lined up. First player passes ball overhead to next player, then peels off and becomes last player. Next player passes and peels off. The entire team must cross the finish line moving backward. Fun stuff! Try it under and under coming back.

CONTINUOUS PASSING RELAY

First player steps out to side of team. All players face first player. On "Go," first player passes to end player, then back to first player - to second - to third - to fourth. When the fourth player passes ball back to first player, the #4 player runs to the up position, and the up player runs to end position. Ball is passed to new #1 player and procedure continues until everyone is back in place.

COOPERATIVE BALL PASSING

Teams of 6 - divide the team into 2 rows of 3. The 2 rows should be about 5 yards apart and face each other. The first two players begin side stepping down to the end line and passing the ball back and forth. Do the same thing back. Set the number of passes that should occur while traveling in one direction.

TIME BOMB

Teams of 5 or 6 are standing in a circle bounce-passing the ball around when the music goes off or whistle blows. The player with the ball stands still. All of the other players run behind player with ball; the ball is passed overhead or between legs (your choice). The last player takes the ball and runs to the front of the line. The first team to do this, wins.

10 FREE THROWS

Teams of 5 are lined up on free throw lines at different baskets. The first player shoots, retrieves the ball, tosses ball to second player; second retrieves, passes to third and gets in line. Each time a free throw is made, the whole team yells, "1 - 2 - 3 - etc." Relay is complete when a total of 10 free throws is made. (Move the line forward for more success.)

RETURN THE BALL RELAY
DRIBBLE, PIVOT, AND PASS RELAY

Teams of 4 are lined up at least 6 feet from other teams. Player #1 dribbles the ball to designated line, 5 - 8 yards away. Player #1 crosses line, pivots and bounce-passes ball to player #2 who must wait behind line until ball arrives. Player #2 dribbles across line, pivots, and passes to #3. When all players are across the line, the relay round is over. Start back the other way.

RETURN TO START RELAYS
PASSING, CATCHING, PIVOTING, DRIBBLING

Players take position as shown in the diagram. On "Go," player #1 passes to #2, pivots, passes to #3. Number 3 pivots, passes to #4. Number 4 dribbles around the cone and back to #1 position. While this is taking place, #1 moves to #2, and so on. Continuous until everyone is back in place.

CIRCLE BALL RELAYS, DRIBBLE AND SHOOT

Four teams of 5 are placed on one court - the other 2 teams are on the half court next to this court; #1 passes to #2, #2 to #3, until #5 receives the ball. When #5 receives the ball, he/she takes off dribbling toward the basket and makes a shot. When he/she makes a shot, the ball is dribbled back to #1 spot and everything starts again. While #5 is shooting, everyone moves over a spot and vacates #1 spot
NOTE: Three attempts and player dribbles ball back.

COMPETITIVE ACTIVITIES - PRACTICE
AROUND THE WORLD

Taking one shot at each station around the key. If a playe makes the shot, he/she moves to next space. A second shot can be taken at the spot where player missed. It is a chance spot. If player misses the second shot, he/she goes back to space one.

BASKETBALL LEAD UP (Continued)

H-O-R-S-E

The objective is to make such great shots that your opponent misses the exact shot that you just made. The first player shoots a shot - the second and third player must make the same shot. If the second player misses, he/she takes an "H." The third player is the new shooter for a shot. Play until opponents are finally out or H-O-R-S-E or 5 misses.

"21"

Each player is attempting to make "21" not "22." First player takes a shot from the free throw line, retrieves ball, takes a shot from that spot, retrieves ball, and takes a shot from that spot. The first shot is worth 5 points, the second shot 3 points, the third shot 1 point. Player totals points for 3 shots. The next player does the same until someone gets 21 points (exact).

Rules to insert (optional):
1. Player must retrieve ball on first bounce.
2. If a player makes all 3 shots, he/she gets another turn right then.

ONE ON ONE - TWO ON TWO - THREE ON THREE

Have students match up with someone about their own ability. This is a half court game which can be played one on one to three on three. The first player or team that scores 20 points wins the half court game.

HOT SPOT SHOOTING

Five mats or spaces are placed near the basket and around the key (same spot everytime). The spots are designated points 1, 2, 3, 4, 5, depending on proximity to basket. Participants are given a time limit to shoot from spots - 1, 2, 3 minutes. Participants retrieve their own shots and shoot again. Total points for scores at end of time limit. (Baskets only.)

FREE THROW CONTEST

Participant stands on free throw line. Three balls and two retriever players are needed. Free throw shooter shoots continuous free throws as retrievers feed the balls one at a time to shooter. Shooter has a 1, 2, or 3 minute time limit. Option: shoot slowly - 10 shots made.

ONE MINUTE SHOOT FROM ANYWHERE

Participant starts shooting from free throw line, retrieves ball, and continues shooting from under the basket for the time limit. Total number of baskets is recorded.

SHUTTLE DRIBBLE FOR TIME

Participant dribbles the length of the court twice, for time. Down and back twice. Stop watch records the time. Fastest time wins.

If possible, use 7" balls; if not, a variety of balls could be used to ensure that each child has a ball. These challenges require 2 minutes of moving and 1 minute of being stationary. Music really helps.

1. Dribble the ball, fingertip control, all over the floor, regular, low dribbles, high dribbles, spins, etc. <u>Preferred Hand</u> - 2 minutes.
<u>One minute task</u> - Stand with feet together, begin moving the ball around ankles, shins, knees, thighs, waist, chest, neck, and head. Go the other way. Spread your feet, push the ball around legs - figure 8 pattern. Just one leg - Faster!

2. Dribble the ball, fingertip control, all over the floor, regular, low dribbles, high dribbles, spins, etc. - other hand - 2 minutes.
<u>One minute task</u> - Butterfly or Quick Hands. Stand with your feet apart, hold the ball between your legs - not touching legs - one hand in front, one hand around a leg. Switch hands as many times as you can without letting the ball hit the floor.

3. Dribble the ball 3 times with your right hand, 3 times with your left hand, as you move. Move in a zig-zag pattern. Imagine that someone is guarding you. Keep your body between the ball and your opponent.
<u>One minute task</u> - Stand and dribble the ball around your body - try to dribble continuously.

4. (Most difficult.) Dribble under a leg while walking forward. Dribbling with right hand, step forward with left leg. Dribble under leg to left hand. Step forward, with right leg, dribble under right leg to right hand. Try to smooth it out.
<u>One minute task</u> - Stand with feet apart. Dribble ball from right hand to left hand through the legs, back and forth, right to left, left to right.

5. Dribble 10 times and move forward rapidly. After the tenth dribble, stop on a dime and catch the ball. Now 10 dribbles with left hand. Stop on a dime. Continue for the 2 minute period.
<u>One minute task</u> - Find a partner. Borrow your partner's ball for one minute. Dribble both balls at the same time. Now, give the balls to your partner - partner's turn.

6. Dribble the ball all over the floor and skip at the same time. Continue for 2 minutes. Try to stay in rhythm.
<u>One minute task</u> - Stand and dribble, go to knees, to sitting, to stomach, to coffee grinder; around once, to sitting, to knees, standing.

7. Dribble the ball all over the floor as you gallop. Switch from side to side if you can. Try to dribble in rhythm - continue for 2 minutes.
<u>One minute task</u> - Find a partner. Develop a fancy passing routine with both balls moving at the same time. Ex: One player bounce-passes the ball, the other player chest-passes the ball.

8. Dribble the ball while sliding in one direction all around the room. After 1 minute, slide in the other direction and change hands. I'll let you know when to change.
<u>One minute task</u> - Stand and dribble while facing me. Keep your eyes on me while you dribble. With your free hand, recreate the letters that I hold up. Now, a new letter.

9. Dribble the ball all over the room while making eye contact with everyone else. "Do not look at the ball." Practice - Practice.
<u>One minute task</u> - Stand in place - toss the ball up, spin your body all the way around and catch the ball on the first bounce. Try it without the bounce.

10. Dribble the ball around the room while imagining that you are in a game situation. Dribble around avoiding other players, changing hands when necessary. Every once in a while, pull up, take a jump shot (like this) but hang on to the ball.
<u>One minute task</u> - Try juggling the ball off of 3 body parts before it hits the ground - head, arms, knees, feet, hands, etc. Try for your top score.

BASKETBALL - SELF TESTING STATIONS

1. <u>Free Throw Shooting</u>
   Pre-season 10 tries _____ shots made
   Post Test 10 tries _____ shots made

2. <u>Shots from Behind the Line</u>
   2 or 3 balls available - 2 returners who feed balls back immediately to shooter. How many shots can you make in 2 minutes from behind the line? Continuous feeding of the ball to shooter.
   Pre-season _____ tries _____ shots made
   Post Test _____ tries _____ shots made

3. <u>Hot Spot Shooting</u>
   Mark the numbers on the blacktop with chalk, or put carpet squares down in the same spot each day. Shoot from the spot, return your own balls. Numbers on the spots are the point values. Use a 3 minute shooting period. Total your points.
   Pre-season _____ points made _____
   Post Test _____ points made _____

4. <u>Around the World</u>
   Take one shot from each around the world spot. The three spaces closest to the basket on each side are worth one point. All of the other spaces are worth 2 or 3 points. Take your shots and total your points.
   Pre-season total points. Final score _____
   Post Test total points. Final score _____

5. <u>Chest Passes Through the Hoop</u>
   Hang a hula hoop from the basketball hoop with a jump rope. Hang it so that the hoop is about chest high. Pass the ball (chest pass) through the hoop from the free throw line. Count the number of chest passes that go through the hoop.
   Pre-season 10 tries _____ passes made
   Post Test 10 tries _____ passes made

6. <u>Chest Bounce Passes Through the Hoop</u>
   Hang a hula hoop from the basketball hoop with a jump rope. <u>Hang</u> it so that the <u>bottom</u> of the hoop is <u>knee high</u>. Pass the ball (bounce pass) through the hoop from the free throw line. Count the number of bounce passes that go through the hoop.
   Pre-season 10 tries _____ passes made
   Post Test 10 tries _____ passes made

7. <u>King/Queen of the Court - Stop Watch</u>
   Dribble begins at end of court between the cones. Stop watch starts. Dribble around A cone to B cone, around end cone or basketball standard and straight back down the court through the cones - elapsed time. A cone and B cone are interchangeable.
   Pre-season elapsed time _____
   Post Test elapsed time _____

8. <u>King/Queen of the Court - Cone Dribble - 10 Cones</u>
   Dribble begins at end of court between the cones or standards. Stop watch starts. He/she dribbles down the court in between each cone, goes through the standards at the end and dribbles straight back to starting point through the cones. Elapsed time.
   Pre-season elapsed time _____
   Post Test elapsed time _____

9. <u>Self Testing 21</u>
   Take one shot from free throw line. Retrieve the ball on the first bounce and shoot from that spot. Return the ball on the first bounce and shoot again. The first shot is worth 5 points; second - 3 points; third - 1 point. Begin at the free throw line again after the third shot
   How many shots did it take to make 21 points?
   Pre-season _____ shots
   Post Test _____ shots

10. <u>Shuttle Dribble for Time - Stop Watch</u>
    Start at the end of the court. Dribble fast to the half court line. Dribble back to start, cross the line, dribble to the end of the court, cross the line, dribble to end of the court, cross line, dribble back.

Pre-season elapsed time _____
Post Test elapsed time _____

11. <u>Shoot 15 Straight Shots or One Minute Time Limit</u>
Stand close to the basket. Shoot a shot, retrieve, shoot, retrieve, shoot
.... No hesitations; stand as close as you can. Shoot 15 continuous shot
How many shots did you make out of 15,
or in one minute?
Pre-season _____ out of 15 shots or one minute
Post Test _____ out of 15 shots or one minute

BASKETBALL DRILLS

Chest Passes   Bounce Passes   Two Ball Passes   Tossing ball overhead
                                                                with both hands

                      Chest Bounce
                         Pass

Lead Passing   Over the Shoulder   Whole Class   Team moves in a
                      Lead Passing   Defense Drill   circle while ball is
                                           player here   being passed around.
   hands up   Players side step -
                       Side Step R or L   Lead the moving
                                           or Back Pedal on   players as you pass...
                                           Command

                              Total Class Drill

Pivoting   Defense   One Hand Set Shot   Lay Up - Jump Shot
Teaching play-   Hands up, Hand   Teacher models   Teacher   Teacher
ers the differ-   nearest the ball   Set Shot - every-   models   models jump
ence between   stretching out -   one follows   lay up.   shot. Every-
pivoting and   Do not over guard.   teacher.   Everyone one follows
walking.   Teacher or student   follows   teacher.
Practice Drill   can lead the group   teacher.
Move - Stop   by dribbling a ball
and Pivot.   from hand to hand
                      and moving from
 side to side.

                      Run Ditto Sheets of Relays - Each Captain Has a Copy
                      Continuous Relays
                      11 3 person teams
                      The 3 person teams run all 10 relays continuously
                      The teacher sets the distance and rules.
                      The first team to complete all 10 relays wins.

              <u>BASKETBALL RELAYS - SHORT DISTANCE - TASK CARD</u>

1. Dribble the ball down and back with your preferred hand.
2. Dribble the ball down and back with other hand.
3. Side step as you dribble the ball down and back with preferred hand.
4. Side step as you dribble the ball down and back with other hand.
5. Skip as you dribble the ball down and back with your preferred hand.
6. Skip as you dribble the ball down and back with other hand.
7. Gallop as you dribble the ball down and back with your preferred hand.
8. Gallop as you dribble the ball down and back with other hand.
9. Make 3 spins as you dribble down, 3 spins back with your preferred hand.
10. Make 3 spins as you dribble down, 3 spins back with other hand.

THE GAME - BASKETBALL

Rules:

1. To start a game, players take positions. Each team has one center, two forwards, and two guards.

2. Play starts as the referee tosses the ball into the air between the two opposing centers in the center circle. The centers attempt to tap the ball to one of their own players.

3. After receiving the ball tapped from the center, the player tries to move the ball toward his/her team's basket by passing it to another player, dribbling it, or using a combination of these actions. To give directions for this activity, it is suggested that the teacher use the formation for offensive play illustrated in the Teaching Suggestions.

4. The opposing team tries to intercept the ball and return it in the direction of its own basket. The ability of the team to intercept the ball can be improved by using the zone defense formation as illustrated in the Teaching Suggestions.

5. The ball may be passed to any player of the team in any section of the court.

6. When the ball goes out-of-bounds, it is given to an opponent of the player who last touched the ball. It is then thrown in to a teammate from the point at which it went out-of-bounds.

7. Any player on the team may shoot for a goal.

8. When a score is made, play is stopped. The ball is then put in play from behind the end line by a guard of the opposing team. The ball is passed to a teammate and play resumes as before.

9. Fouls: Any player who trips, pushes, holds, charges, or has unnecessary body contact with an opponent is charged with a foul.

   Penalty: One or two free throws.

   A. If a player is fouled when engaged in play other than shooting, one free throw is awarded that player at the free-throw line. If the free throw is unsuccessful, the ball is in play.
   B. When a player is fouled while actually shooting, two free throws are awarded the fouled player at the free-throw line. If the second free throw is unsuccessful, the ball is in play.

10. Violations: A violation is charged when any player takes more than one step with the ball without dribbling (traveling), double dribbles the ball, steps on or over a boundary line while in possession of the ball, kicks the ball, causes the ball to go out-of-bounds, or delays the game by keeping the ball in his/her possession for more than five seconds while closely guarded.

    Penalty: Play is stopped, and the referee gives the ball to an opposing player, who puts it in play from out-of-bounds, nearest the point of infraction, by passing it to a teammate.

Shoulder Pass- Both Hands

Volleyball Leadup Activities

And Other Court Games

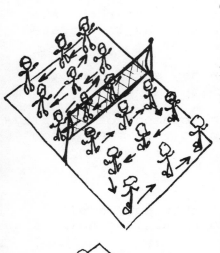

NET BALL

Teams are divided (2) equally. One team serves by throwing the ball over the net from the right back corner. The ball is caught by a player on the opposing team, he/she throws it to another player, the ball is caught and thrown to another player. The third player to touch the ball throws it over the net. The same procedure follows until someone misses. NOTE: Tell your students that the ball is a hot potato, and they must get rid of it as fast as they receive it. (Call time on people who hold the ball over two seconds.) The ball cannot be returned to the person who tosses it to another person on his/her side.

Example: 1-2-1 - Lost ball or point
1-2-6 - Three different people to handle the ball before it is returned.

Points are awarded only if your team is serving. If the serving team misses, they lose their serve, not a point. Game can be played to 15 or 21 points with one point awarded for each volley that is won by the serving team.

LOW NET NEWCOMB

Teams of 5 are placed on the back half of each side of the court. Ball is put in play by a player in the back line throwing the ball across the net. The object of the game is to throw the ball hard within bounds so the opposing players can't catch the ball. Each team must have 3 players touch the ball before it can be thrown across the net. A completely missed ball must land in bounds to score a point for the other team. Only the serving team can score a point. VARIATIONS: Use a Nerf football and pass the ball. Make this game Chest Pass Low Net Newcomb.

BOUNDARY BALL

Teams of 5 are placed on the court with cones dividing the center. Team may play 3 players in court and 2 players beyond the back line for retrieval purposes. The object of the game is for a player to stop the ball, run forward to the center line, smash it down inside the opposing court, and make it bounce once outside the court. (One bounce inside, one bounce outside scores 1 point.) The retrievers attempt to keep the ball from bouncing out, and they feed the ball to the up players. The ball must bounce in Fair Territory out of bounds.

VOLLEYBALL LEAD UP (Continued)

SCOOP BASKETBALL BOMBARDMENT
A volleyball net divides the basketball court into two
equal sides. Students are divided into two teams, and each
student has a plastic scoop. Distribute to both teams 20 to
25 Wiffle Balls or Tennis Balls. On signal, each player
attempts to launch the ball in his/her scoop over the volleyball net and into the stacked up trash can on the other side.
All loose balls are caught or picked up and launched. Ropes
are put around the trash cans to make an off-limits area -
prevents goal tending. Balls can be picked up in roped off
area.
NOTES: Lower the net and move the trash cans up for the
lower grades. Trash cans come from behind the kitchen.

DECK RING TENNIS BOMBARDMENT
Teams are placed on the court. Play begins with the whistle. One, two, or three deck rings can be used, depending
on the skill of the players. All tosses over the net must
be underhand tosses. The object of the game is to score
points by playing so well that your opponents drop or miss
the rings. One point is awarded to the opposing team when
a ring touches the ground on one side.
VARIATION: Catch Up Deck Ring Tennis Bombardment. See
Catch Up Ball.

SERVE IT BASEBALL - VOLLEYBALL
Players are divided into 2, 5, 6, or 7-person teams. One
team serves, the other catches. The object of the game is
for a player from the serving team to hit the ball inbounds
(over the net and inside the court) and run around the cone
by the net and back to the serving area before players from
the other team catch the ball and line up. After the ball
is hit inbounds, the receiving team runs inside their half
of the court and tries to catch the ball. When the ball is
caught, the other players on the team line up in back of
the catcher, and the ball is passed overhead until it reaches
the last player in line. If the last player reaches the
front of the line before the runner is back between his/her
cones, the runner is out. If the runner beats, his team
scores. A ball hit out of bounds (not over the net or out
of court) is a foul; three fouls and server is out. After
all players on one team have served, teams change sides of
court. Players serve until a served ball is called dead,
or players foul out.

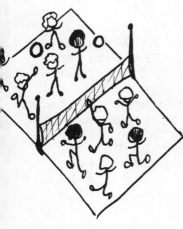

CATCH UP BALL
Teams of 5 players are placed on each side of the court. A
low net or chairs divide the court. Each team begins with
one ball. The object of the game is to force the other team
to have two balls in possession (in hand) at the same time.
One point is scored each time that this happens. (Two
players on the same team are holding balls at the same time.)
Players catch and get rid of the ball rapidly. Eleven
points make a game.

VOLLEYBALL LEAD UP (Continued)

FRISBEE VOLLEY, SHOOT AND CATCH

Teams of 6 are placed on each side of the court. The game begins with each team serving 2 frisbees from anywhere behind their line. The object of the game is to keep the flight low, throw correctly, and score points for your team. One point is awarded for each tin can or object knocked down by the frisbee. Three points are awarded when the object in the hoop is knocked down. Objects can be set up on waste baskets turned upside down.

HERCULES BALL

Teams of 5 are placed on each side of the court. The Earth-ball is put in play by having one team throw the ball over the net. The object of the game is to make the Earthball bounce twice on one side. A point is awarded if the ball bounces twice on one side. Immediately throw the ball over after a point is awarded. Continuous play.

THREE FLIES UP IN A HOOP

Players are placed on the court standing in their hoops. The server serves the ball over the net. Players in hoops can go after the ball and catch it provided they do not step out of the hoop. They may slide hoop around with their feet. The first player to catch 3 flies, goes up and becomes the server.

LOW NET BOUNCE VOLLEY BALL

Teams are placed on the court and are set up to play the same way a six-man volleyball team would be organized. The server bounces the ball, hits it over the net, and the ball must bounce in court. The opposing player bumps the ball and lets the ball bounce; another team player volleys the ball for one bounce; the next team player volleys the ball over the net.
RULE: A ball must bounce 3 times on each side before it is returned.
The serving team receives 1 point for a score, and the opposing team can only earn the serve back.
NOTE: Lead up without the net could promote more success.

PRISON BALL

Divide playing field into 3 parts - a neutral territory in the center, 4 yards wide, and 2 end courts which may be adjusted in size according to the number of players. Each team has a prison on the side of its court. The ball is started by a player on one team who calls the name of a player on the opposite team and throws the ball across neutral ground into the opponents' court. The opponents must catch the ball before it hits the ground in their court or player whose name was called must go to the other team's prison. Any player on the team may catch the ball. If it is caught, the catcher calls an opponent's name and throws it into the opponent's court. A team may free a prisoner by calling the prisoner's name as the ball is thrown into the opponents' court. If the ball is not caught by the opponents, the prisoner may return to his/her own team.

VOLLEYBALL LEAD UP (Continued)

BALLOON VOLLEYBALL

Teams of 5 are placed on court. Between 3 and 5 balloons are used to begin the game, depending on the level of the students. The object of the game is to keep the balloons up and in play. If any balloon lands on your court, a score is given to the opposing team. When a balloon falls, count the point and put it back in play. Continuous play.
VARIATION: Beach Ball Volleyball

SHOWER BALL

The game starts by one team throwing 3 - 6 balls over the net simultaneously from the back line. The opponents attempt to keep the balls from hitting the ground by catching them and throwing them back across the net. No player may hold the ball more than 3 seconds. Taking more than one step with the ball is not allowed. The player catching the ball may not pass to a teammate; he/she must return the ball over the net quickly. A point is scored when the ball hits the ground or goes out-of-bounds. After the score, the player nearest the ball puts it in play by throwing it over the net. A game consists of 21 points.

TOTAL CLASS DRILLS BY THE TEACHER

Students will not understand anticipation and going to the ball unless the teacher takes time to work through this drill.

Teacher holds the ball. If he/she holds ball stretched out in the right hand, all players slide left; left hand, all players slide right; out in front, all players back up; down by feet, all players move forward with hands held low.
NOTE: Students need to be taught to move and reach for the ball.

VOLLEYBALL LEAD UP (Continued)

GAME: VOLLEYBALL LEAD UP DRILLS
AREA: BLACKTOP
EQUIPMENT: VOLLEYBALL

SHUTTLE TOSS

KEEP IT UP
(Variation - One
Bounce in Between)

KEEP IT UP
Players keep moving
around circle.

KEEP IT UP
Against the wall.
First player hits
it high, next player
hits it up.

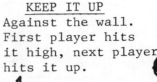

KEEP IT UP
FOUR SQUARE

Serve a square for
points. 15 points
wins. Player in be-
tween can stop ball
if serve isn't arching.

NET RETURN RELAYS
Two or more teams
are lined up in front
of volleyball net.
Leaders stand on other
side of net and toss
ball over net to players.
Every returned volley
counts as one point.

BOUNCE SHUTTLE RELAY
Two or more teams line
up in shuttle formation.
A-1 tosses ball up so
that it lands in middle,
bounces upward - A-2
volleys ball on first
bounce to A-3. Then
moves to back of oppo-
site line. When every-
one is back in place
the relay is over.

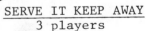

ZIGZAG RELAYS
Can be throwing and
catching, serving, set
yourself up and volley,
etc. Leader serves
straight across, next
player serves to right.
Ball returns same way.
When leader has ball
again the relay is
over.

SET UP PRACTICE
Player #2 sets up player
#1 - #1 volleys ball over
net to #3 - #3 returns
ball under net to #2
player. 3 volleys by #2
and then everyone rotates.

SERVE IT KEEP AWAY
3 players
Player #1 and #3 serve the
ball to each other - #2
player attempts to inter-
cept. If #2 intercepts,
he/she takes the place of
#1.

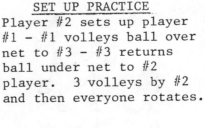

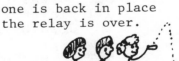

VOLLEYBALL RULES

PROCEDURE:

Volleyball is played across a high net by two teams made up of from one to nine players. The object of the game is to control the ball by volleying (batting with the fingers) on one side and returning it to the opponents' court in such a way that the latter team cannot return the ball. Points are won only by the serving team. A player is required to serve the ball from behind the right end line without assistance from teammates. For in-experienced players, a service position may be used from 5 to 15 feet from the net at the center of each court. Each member of each team serves in turn as numbered. Following each successful service, the server steps into the court and helps with the volleying. The server continues his/her serve until his/her side makes a mistake and loses the serve.

TERMS:

Serving Team	– Team serving ball
Receiving or Service-	Team receiving the ball
Serving or Service	– Act of stricking the ball after each point
Side Out	– When serving team loses its service and the ball goes to the receiving team (no point is scored)
Volley	– The process of batting the ball back and forth over the net after service and before an error is made (sometimes called a rally)
Let Ball	– A ball that clips the top of the net and falls into the opponents' court
Net Ball	– A ball that strikes into the net
Dead Ball	– A ball that does not score because of some violation by either team.
Fair Ball	– A ball which strikes any boundary line of either court so close to the net that it cannot be returned
Setting Up the Ball -	Playing the ball so that it will be in position for a forward to drive over the net

SERVED BALL:

The value of a served ball is determined by one of three conditions that may prevail following the service:

1. Fair Ball   A serve is fair ball if the ball is:

    A. Correctly served and it clears the net and falls to the ground within or on a boundary line of the opposing court, or

    B. It is legally contacted by a member of the opposing team.

Softball Leadup Activities

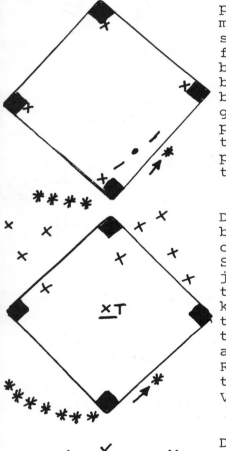

BASE RUN - BEAT THE BALL

An activity devised for 6-8 players. There are always 4
players in the field - one player at each base. The remaining players are up to run. The base runner and the
softball start at the same time. The catcher throws to
first and around the bases. The catcher must throw the
ball around the bases twice while the runner circles the
bases once. One point is scored if the runner beats the
ball. After one team runs, teams exchange places. If the
game is played on a work up basis with an uneven number of
players, the field players work their way up by playing
third base, second base, first base, and catcher. The out
player goes to third base, and the catcher becomes one of
the up players.

MARATHON SOFTBALL

Divide the players into 2 equal teams. Play regular softball rules, except that teams do not change places after 3
outs. They change places after 3, 4, or 5 minutes of play.
Set the limit. Count the runs, not the outs. It is the
job of the up team to stay organized and ready to bat. The
teacher has 3 balls at the mound. The teacher's job is to
keep pitching the balls after outs and fouls in order to
turn the batting line over as many times as possible within
the time limit. As soon as the time is up, the teacher
announces the score, and the other team begins their time up.
RULE: One wiff strike or two foul balls make an out; turn
the lines over.
VARIATION: Play Marathon Tennis Baseball. It's Wild!

LONG BASE SOFTBALL

Divide the players into 2 equal teams. Up players can hit
the ball and run to first or first and back home. Running
rule: Players can stay at first until 3 players stack up
at first, then everyone must run on the next hit regardless
of how good the hit is. Players can be put out by (1) first
base being tagged by a player with the ball before the
hitter-runner gets there, or (2) being tagged with the ball
while running.
NOTES: Four runs can be scored on one hit. Three outs
could be made on one hit or play. Encourage field players
to throw the ball carefully. Change sides after 3 outs.
Do not throw the ball away and let everyone score!

The game is played with the same rules that are used for softball with a few exceptions. The batter uses a tennis racquet for a bat, the pitcher uses tennis balls to pitch, and some of the fielders can use scoops to catch fly balls (optional).

NOTES: This equipment is very adaptable to use for playing Marathon Tennis Baseball. See Marathon Softball. Lots of action! One wiff strike or two foul balls make an out in Marathon Tennis Baseball. Turn the lines over - the teacher pitches.

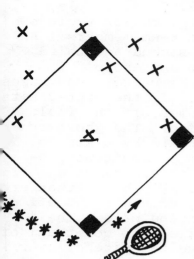

ROTATION SOFTBALL

This game is played exactly like regulation softball except players rotate positions after each inning. This game is highly recommended as it gives children practice in playing all positions.

VARIATIONS: Players in field rotate positions after each out.

TEACHER SUGGESTIONS: Explain to class why it is important for all participants to have the opportunity of playing each position. Explain that lesser skilled players need class support and encouragement so that they also get an opportunity to develop some confidence.

PICKLE ACTIVITY

Pickle is an activity devised for 3-5 players in a group. The object of the activity is to provide an opportunity for players to practice throwing, catching, and base running skills under pressure. Set 2 bases down the normal distance between 2 bases on the field. A player with a glove is stationed at each base. The runner is tagged up on one of the bases. The glove players begin playing catch. The runner takes off at an opportune moment and tries to run to the other base. The field players attempt to get the runner into a run down or "pickle" situation and tag him/her out. If tagged, the runner takes a glove and a glove player becomes a runner. Two or three runners give everyone a chance to take a breather.

THREE FLIES UP ACTIVITY

A batter is up. All other players are fielders and take turns about catching flies. When a player catches 3 flies, he/she becomes the batter.

BOOMER BAT BASEBALL

This game is played with the same rules as softball except for a few exceptions. A soft liter bottle with a dowel for a handle is used for the bat. See Striking Tools. A 4, 5, 6, or 7" Red Ball is used in place of softballs. The pitcher can pitch the ball with one bounce or no bounce. The ball really booms when it is hit. Great action!

STRIKE BALL

The game is played with the same rules that are used for softball with a few exceptions. A Volleyball or Red ball is used for the game. The striker (up player) must strike the ball out of his/her hand or bounce the ball off of home plate and strike it with his/her fist. If the ball is caught in the air, an out is made. A base runner cannot leave base before the ball is socked. Change sides after everyone has been up to strike. Count the runs, not the outs.

VARIATION: Play Work Up Strike Ball.

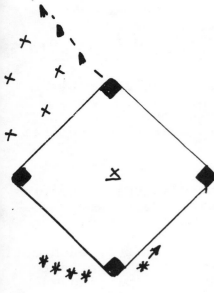

OVER THE LINE ACTIVITY

Over the Line can be played with 6, 7, 8, 9, or 10 players. Teams are divided evenly. Team players pitch for their own teams and attempt to make hitters out of team members. An arbitrary straight line is used between second and third base. The ball must be hit into the air and dropped in safely over the line to become a hit. The batter runs bases until the ball is thrown to the pitcher. If the batter hits a double, he/she touches second, then comes off the field because he/she will need to bat again soon. The ghost runner is still at second and is moved to third by a single. A double will bring the ghost runner home. Don't worry - your students will keep track of "whose on first."

If a grounder is hit, the batter is out. Fly balls that are caught are outs. The ball must be hit into the coned off side of the field on the left side of second base. The 4 field players are stationed out in the field to cover all of the area that is in fair territory. Move the pitcher over toward the third base line when a left handed batter is up to bat.

FAT BAT WIFFLE BALL SOFTBALL (Success)

Use a fat plastic bat that can be purchased inexpensively at Gemco, K Mart, Payless, etc. The game is played with the same rules as softball except that players use _fat bats_ and _plastic wiffle balls_. A very success oriented game - especially for primary children and players with limited skills - just fun to play anyway!

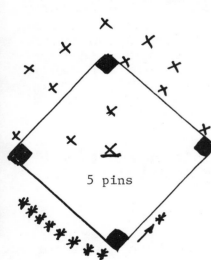

HIT THE PIN SOFTBALL

Divide into 2 equal teams. Play rules of softball except the player who hits the ball runs the bases while the opposing team tries to knock over the bowling pins (placed on a shorter base line) before the runner reaches home. NOTE: Use 5 pins third, short second, short first. The order of hitting the pins is not important. Keep the same team up until everyone has had a chance to hit. Count the runs, not the outs. Set pins inside of bases so that runners will not get tangled up with the pins. Pins are knocked down by touching them with the ball.

NOTE: Emphasize teamwork; 5 people must touch the ball while knocking the pins down. Keep 2 balls in game to avoid delays when one ball is out of play. Adjust success by changing bases and pins.

5 pins

DANISH ROUNDER SOFTBALL

Divide players into 2 equal teams. Play rules of home run softball. The hitter hits the pitched ball into the field of play. He/she then runs around his/her lined up teammates as many times as he/she can before a player in the field can retrieve the ball, throw it to another player, have that player throw it to another, and then tag home plate. The runner scores a run each time he/she circles his/her lined up teammates.

NOTE: The ball must be touched by either 3, 4, or 5 players in the field before it comes home. Decide before the game. Keep the same team up until everyone has hit the ball. Count runs, not outs. Emphasize teamwork. Keep two balls in game to avoid delays.

Wind Mill

Right hand to left toe. Stand straight. Left hand to right toe.

Physical Fitness Activities
Strength
Endurance
Flexibility

Arm Circles

Big circles, small circles. Forward-backward.

Leg Stretch

Step out far enough to feel your leg stretch. Step out with left leg - stand straight - step out with right leg. Reach around leg with both hands on stretch.

Toe Toucher

Touch toes. Keep legs straight, feet together. Return to starting position.

Warm Up Activities
Stretching

Step Out Leg Extension

stretch forward and backward slowly. Change legs.

side   Back   side   Forward

Lariat: stretch-stretch-stretch

Body Bender

Side Way Over   Up   Side Way Over

Heel-Toe Raise

Move up on toes - hold. Move back on heels - hold.

Back Stretcher

Reach back between your legs as far as you can.

Foot Pull

Stand on one foot. Bend knee of other leg and pull foot upward. Change sides.

Foot Circles

Rotate foot in all directions. Change sides.

Can you Keep up with me for one minute?

On your stomachs, on your side, your other side, up running in place, on your back, on your seat, on your back, two situps, up bicycling, stand up, sit down, on your side, on your Knees, up running in place, hit the deck, log roll to your right 3 times, sit up, lay down on your stomach, push up and clap hands, on all fours, on your back, up bicycling, stand up, jump up and down 3 times, 4 jumping jacks, touch your toes, sit down, yell "Yuck!", on your side, coffee grinder position, body around, collapse, standup, spin, sit down, lay down, rest.

Endurance Activities

Exercise in place continuously until the record stops.

Circuit Training
Use records to move and change stations.

Push Ups, Hoop sloop, Jump Rope, Squat Jumps, Windmills, Chair Dips

Start with 15-20 seconds of exercise at each station with 5-10 seconds of rest between stations. Decrease rest periods and increase exercise period.

Aerobic
Moving to music. Change activity continuously until record stops. Jogging, running, fast running, hopping, jumping, run backwards, skip, leap, gallop, skip backwards, change change.
3 minutes of activity, one minute of rest. Increase activity time.

Multi-purpose Room
Obstacle Course
Obstacle in rows (set up by students) Start with follow the leader, then move to the entire circuit.
Change leaders. Use records.

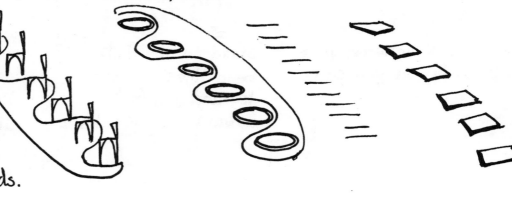

Chair Push Up

Feet against wall, chair 14-18" above floor. The body must be kept straight. Continuous push ups. Practice the test often.

Flexed Arm Hang

Stop watch starts as soon as soon as participant is in hanging position. Practice the test often.

Bar Dips - Parallel Bars

Start in front support position on parallel bars. Dip, feet do not make any contact with ground. Return to starting position.

Arm Strength Activities

Peg Board

Put pegs in holes. Climb higher.

Pull Up

Use forward grip. Raise body up until your chin is above bar. Lower body to a full hang or to starting position. Practice the test often.

Chair Dips
Feet out in front. Push yourself up, let yourself down.

Isometric Wall Push

Push against wall, hold for 15 seconds, release, hold... Try finger tip push.

Tetherball Pole climb for time. Climb 3 poles and touch the top.

Low Bar Modified Pull Up

Body straight and under bar.

Individual Tug-of-War Ropes

Right hands, left hands, both hands pull across.

Crab Walk

Walk around floor to line. Crab soccer. Crab relays.

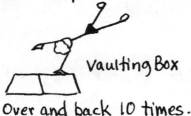

Vaulting Box

Over and back 10 times.

Multi-purpose Room rope climb.

Forearm Push Up

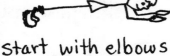

Start with elbows even with ears, forearms on mat. Push up, back straight.

Sideways Roll Over

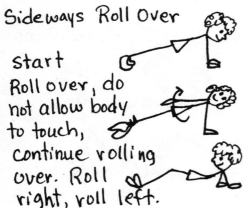

start
Roll over, do not allow body to touch, continue rolling over. Roll right, roll left.

Travel Ladder

Jump Rope

Pull and hold for 15 seconds. Release Repeat...

Push Up

start- back straight, head up, lower body keeping a straight line from head to feet.

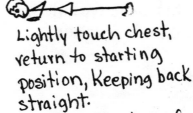

Lightly touch chest, return to starting position, keeping back straight.
1. Improve number of pushups.
2. Walk sideways
3. Seal Crawl- drag body forward.

Finger Tip Push Ups

Push off finger tips.

Coffee Grinder

Right spin, left spin, 360° on each hand.

Arm Wrestling

Wheelbarrow

Seal Clap

start in push up position

Push with hands, spring into air and clap hands. Return to starting position.

Widespread Push Up

start in push up position with arms spread to the side. Push up, keep back straight, hips level.

Standing Long Jump

Stretch body before jumping. Begin with arms down and back. Jump forward swinging arms forcefully forward and upward. Practice the test often. Work on form.

Side Step

center line

Begin by straddling center line. On signal slide to your left, step on or cross line for one point. Slide right, cross center for second point. Continue right, step on or cross line for third point . . . ten seconds.

Leg Strength Activities

Jump Rope
Consecutive jumps.

Squat Jumps
Spring upward from the floor, change forward foot. Land - spring . . .

Step Test

Face Chair #1. Step up onto chair once, step down. Move over. Step up and down on Chair #2 twice. Move over. Step up and down on chair #3 three times. Continue. Begin with four or five chairs, work up to seven. Practice.

Running Broad Jump

Land on the mat. Measure the distance.

Paper Bag Jump

Brackets
0-5
6-10
11-15
16-20
21-25
26-30
31-35

Stand beside your paper bag. Jump over the bag sideways with continuous jumping. Get yourself into a "Bracket" and try to improve your score.

Back to Back Combinations
Push opponent across line.

Push opponent off mat.

Down the Mat Jumps

Bouncing Ball

Relays

Try for the fewest number of jumps to reach the end.

Modified Sit Up

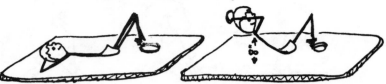

Torso moves off of the mat 8"
and then back down.

Sitting Tucks

Lean back and
raise legs 12".

Pull chest to knees. Reverse
order. Do not let feet touch
the mat.

Leg Lifts

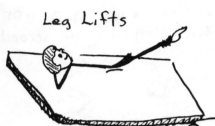

Lie on back.
Pull straight legs
6" off the mat
and hold in position
for 10 seconds.
Repeat . . .

Abdominal Strength Activities

Flutter Kick

Lie on back. Kick legs
as in swimming.

V Sit

Lie on mat.

Knee Bent Situp

Lie on back, knees bent,
feet flat on mat.

Raise both head and
feet at the same time.
Legs straight, arms
straight to sides.

Sit up, touch elbows to
knees.

117

Super Rubberband Activities

stretching
1. Side to side
2. Trunk twist

Pull tight in front, count to 10.

Hold behind neck.
1. Pull tight
2. Trunk twist

Partners contract legs.

Partners
1. Rocking
2. Pulling back

Ankle stretch farther apart.

Sitting leg stretch.

Side leg stretch, raise top leg.

Arm pump. Pump arms up and down.

Tug of war.

Rooster Fight. Make opponent put foot down.

Hold behind back
1. Count to ten.
2. Body twist.

Four way tug of war. Loop 4 rubber bands together.

Siamese Tag

Siamese Clean Your Own Backyard.

Siamese Relays

Six ball Siamese tag soccer.

Step through and back.

Leg stretch extend.

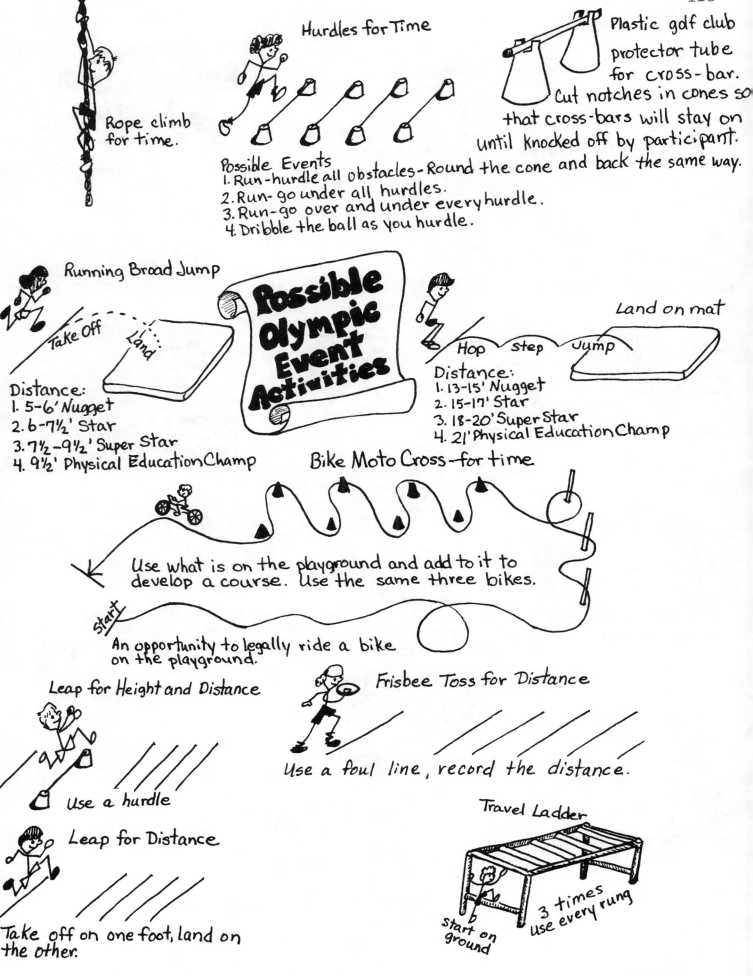

Rope climb for time.

Hurdles for Time

Plastic golf club protector tube for cross-bar. Cut notches in cones so that cross-bars will stay on until knocked off by participant.

Possible Events
1. Run-hurdle all obstacles-Round the cone and back the same way.
2. Run- go under all hurdles.
3. Run- go over and under every hurdle.
4. Dribble the ball as you hurdle.

Running Broad Jump

Take Off   Land

Distance:
1. 5-6' Nugget
2. 6-7½' Star
3. 7½-9½' Super Star
4. 9½' Physical Education Champ

Possible Olympic Event Activities

Hop   step   Jump

Land on mat

Distance:
1. 13-15' Nugget
2. 15-17' Star
3. 18-20' Super Star
4. 21' Physical Education Champ

Bike Moto Cross -for time

Use what is on the playground and add to it to develop a course. Use the same three bikes.

Start

An opportunity to legally ride a bike on the playground.

Leap for Height and Distance

Use a hurdle

Frisbee Toss for Distance

Use a foul line, record the distance.

Leap for Distance

Take off on one foot, land on the other.

Travel Ladder

start on ground

3 times use every rung

High Jump Standards (3 Events)

 1.

 2.

 3.

1. Limbo! How low can you go! Warm up, stretch before this event. Record the height of the bar.

2. Limbo Dribble! Non-stop. How low can you go while continually dribbling the ball as you go under the bar?

3. High Jump. Use four or five mats for landing.

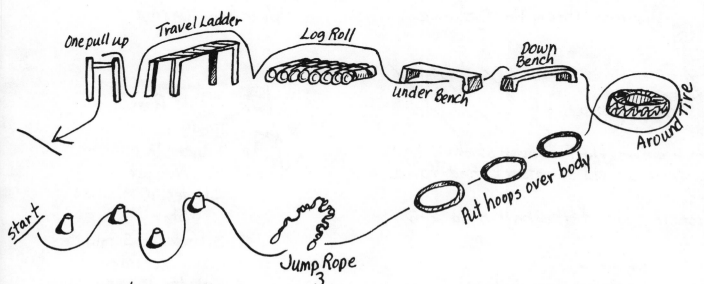

Physical Fitness Challenge Course.-Can be designed by the class.

Six Minute Jog-Walk

10 Quarters = Nugget
11 Quarters = Star
12 Quarters = Super Star
13 Quarters (Girls) = Physical Education Champ
14 Quarters (Boys) = Physical Education Champ

Mat Distance Activities for Time

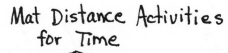
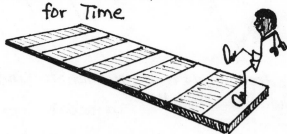

Hit only on everyother section.
1. Jumping
2. Hopping
3. Sideways Hopping
4. Log Rolls
5. Animal Walks: crab, kangaroo, lame dog, seal, commando, creep.

Discus Throw for Distance

stay in hoop or circle.

Indoor: Two Frisbees taped together.
Outdoor: Two Frisbees taped together with rope coiled up inside to add weight.

Hammer Throw for Distance

Spin 360°
Stay in hoop or circle.

Indoor: Use two fluff or nylon stocking balls stuffed into an old sweatsock tied to a 2' cord.
Outdoor: Use the tetherball on a 2-3' cord.

Shot Put for Distance

Push the shot

Foul Line

Indoor: Fluff ball or Nylon stocking ball
Outdoor: Softball

Baskeball Court Run

Take times for entire class, then divide class into levels.

Finish   Start

100 Yard Dash

Times
1. Under 22 seconds = Nugget
2. Under 20 seconds = Star
3. Under 18 seconds = Superstar
4. Under 16 seconds = Physical Education Champ.

Mile Run

Times
1. Under 12 minutes
   Nugget
2. Under 10 minutes
   Star
3. Under 8.5 minutes
   Superstar
4. Under 7 minutes
   Physical Education Champ

50 Yard Dash

Times
1. Under 10.5 seconds
   Nugget
2. Under 9.8 seconds
   Star
3. Under 8.5 seconds
   Superstar
4. Under 8.0 seconds
   Physical Education Champ

Other Events
Gallop
Slide
Skip

Run Backward
Dribble Ball
Jump Rope

Zig-Zag Agility Run or Dribble

set up cones exactly the same way each day. Use a stopwatch.

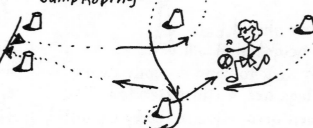

Can be:
Running, Dribbling,
Soccer Dribbling,
Jump Roping.

King/Queen of the Court for Time. Players take off at one end of the court and travel as fast as possible around the cones and back through the starting gates for time. Use a stopwatch.

10-12-15 yds.

Shuttle Run For Time. Players take off on one end and follow the pattern around the cones. Players will need to practice turns and develop their own method of turning corners. Use a stopwatch.
Note: Erasers can be picked up and carried back and placed across line.

Throw For Distance

Indoor: Fluff Ball, Yarn Ball, Nylon Stocking Ball
Outdoor: Softball
1. 50-70' Nugget
2. 71-90' Star
3. 91-100' SuperStar
4. 100+' Physical Education Champ

Javelin Throw for Distance

Indoor javelin: Golfclub protector tube with a little foam stuffed and taped into one end.
Outdoor javelin: Dowel with a piece of hose or tubing 8" long placed on one end for weight.

Maze Ball Dribbling
Cones 5-6' apart.
Mark the floor so that the cones can be set on the same spot each day. Use the same type of ball and a stopwatch. Use 8 to 10 cones.

Pull Up

The bar should be at a height that will permit you to hang so your arms and legs are fully extended. Use forward grip. Raise body up until chin is above bar. Lower body to a full hang or to starting position.

Flexed Arm Hang

Two spotters (one in front, one in back) help participants into a raised position. Chin is above but not over the bar, elbows flexed. Chest is close to bar. Stopwatch starts as soon as participant is in hanging position. Stop the watch as soon as
1. Chin touches bar or
2. Head tilts backward or
3. Player's chin falls below bar level.

Chair Push Up

The body must be kept straight. Use a chair that has a seat measuring from 14-18 inches above the ground. No time limit, continuous push ups.

Side Step

Begin by straddling center line. On signal slide to your left, step on or across line for one point. Slide right, cross center for second point. Continue right, step on or across line for third point. Continue for 10 seconds. Lines are 4 feet apart about 5 feet long.

Knee Bent Sit Up for Time

Curl up, touch knees with elbows, return to the floor. Count the number of correctly executed sit ups in 60 seconds.

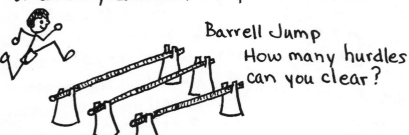

Barrell Jump
How many hurdles can you clear?

Punt for Distance and Accuracy

Girls	Boys
1. 9-11 yds. = Nugget	1. 15-18 yds. = Nugget
2. 12-13 yds. = Star	2. 19-22 yds. = Star
3. 14-15 yds. = Super Star	3. 23-24 yds. = Super Star
4. 16+ yds. = Physical Education Champ	4. 25+ = Physical Education Champ

Pass for Distance and Accuracy

Girls	Boys
1. 10-13 yds. = Nugget	1. 15-19 yds. = Nugget
2. 14-17 yds. = Star	2. 20-23 yds. = Star
3. 18-19 yds. = Super Star	3. 24-25 yds. = Superstar
4. 20+ yds. = Physical Education Champ	4. 26+ yds. = Physical Education Champ

Directions

Whether punting, passing or place kicking is taking place, the actual distance that the ball travels on the fly from the starting line until it hits the ground is measured. An adjustment is made for distance away from the line.

Example

If the ball is thrown 50' and lands 5' off of the line, the distance awarded is 45'. Forty-five points would be given the participant if it was the best throw. Add those points to the total.

Place Kick for Distance and Accuracy

75 Yard Dash

Times
1. Under 14 seconds
   Nugget
2. Under 13 seconds
   Star
3. Under 12 seconds
   Superstar
4. Under 11 seconds
   Physical Education Champ

Soccer Ball Fitness Dribble

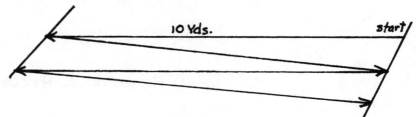

10 Yds.   start

Three Tether Ball Pole Climb for Time

start   Finish

Climb each pole, touch
the top, slide down, go
to next pole, run to finish
line.

Soccer Ball Cone Dribbling

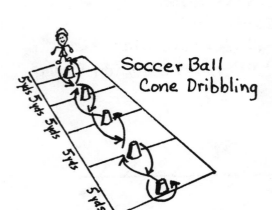

5 yds 5 yds 5 yds 5 yds 5 yds

Bike Snail Race for Time

How long will it take you
to travel the distance? Go as
slow as you can without putting
your foot down. Use the same bike
for everyone.

Step Test for Time

Face Chair #1, step up on chair _once_,
step down. Move over, step up and
down on chair #2 _twice_. Move over,
step up and down on Chair #3 _three_
times. Continue with 4 or 5 chairs.
Work up to seven chairs. Use benches
or Kindergarten chairs against a wall.
Use a stop watch.

Standing Long Jump

stretch body before jumping. Begin
with your arms down and back. Jump
forward swinging your arms forcefully
ahead and upward.

Combatives

Combatives are a natural activity for children. They love to put their new found strength and arts against each other.

Combatives can be tied in with other mat activities such as stunts and tumbling, presented as a theme unit, or as a station along with other activities. Safe, fair, individual competition is an integral part of any program when children are ready.

Recommended for Grades 3, 4, 5, and 6.

Use individual tug-of-war ropes. Reach back and pick up the object 10 inches behind you.

Stick Twist
Facing each other 12" apart, grasp stick with overhand grip. Player wins when opponent is forced to change grip.

Thumb Wrestle
Grip right hands (or left). Press thumbs together and on signal separate thumbs. Try to pin opponent's thumb for a three count.

Hand Slap
The object of this activity is for the palms-up player to quickly slap the hand or hands of the palms-down player.

Noose Caboose
Place the hose loop around your waist. Attempt to back up and pull opponent across line

Bull Dog Pull
Use tug-of-war ropes. Reach back and pickup the object 10" behind you.

SuperBand Tug-of-War
Pull your opponent across the line. Use double Super Rubber Bands.

Rat Tails
Step on your opponent's rope and make it fall to the ground.

Team Tug-of-War
Pull your opponents across the line.

Two individual tug of-war ropes

Four Way Tug-of-War

Four super rubber bands.
Pull your opponent across the line.

Tire Push - Pull Out
Opponents face each other
while standing inside bicycle
tires. On signal players push,
pull, or fake in order to force
opponent to step out of tire.

Tire Drag Across
Opponents stand inside a
26" bicycle tire facing each
other, hands gripping the
sides. On signal each tries to
drag opponent backward to line.

Hand Wrestle
Pull opponent all the way
across line.

Hand Twist
Facing each other, opponents
lock middle fingers of right
hand. Play wins when he
forces opponent's palm upward.

Ring Push
With arms folded
across chest, opponents
try to force each other
to step out of circle.

Back-to-Back Push Across
Opponents (back-to-back) try
to push each other across
the line.

Back-to-Back Pull Across
Lock elbows, push or pull
opponent across a line 3'
from center.

Palm Push - Fake Push
Contestants stand facing
each other, palms held about
1" apart. On signal push or
fake a push or pull to force
a move of the foot.

Two Hand Push or Pull Across
Pull or push opponent across line
3' from center.

Elbow Pull Across
Same side. Opposite side

Rope Jousting
Players begin on a low board with rope in hand. They joust until one person runs out of rope or steps down.

Pillow Push
Opponents push each other with pillows while standing on a 2"x4" board, until one person steps down.

Stump Pull Off
Opponents balance on one foot and try to pull the other person off balance.

Bean Bag Grab
Opponents sit with hands on hips. On signal they reach for beanbag. Either player - or neutral player- calls for right, left, or two hand grab.

Tennis Ball - Rhythm Stick Hockey
Opponents hit a tennis ball back and forth with rhythm sticks. The ball must stay between legs or opponent receives a point.

Billy Bull
Begin on knees in the middle of a mat. With a pillow, push your opponent until a body part touches the floor.

Arm Wrestle
Opponents begin face down on the mat. Arm wrestle, two attempts right hand, two attempts left hand.

Crab Contest
Both contestants in crab position with seats held high. On signal they jostle and push until one touches seat down or touches off mat.

Grab the Flag
Players remain on knees and try to grab opponent's flag.

Bulldozer
Opponents start on hands and feet, facing each other, shoulders touching. Contestants try to push (not bump) each other until one touches a body part to the floor or is pushed across the line.

Leg Wrestling
Opponents begin flat on their backs, feet to head, hips even. Raise left leg three times, on count of three, hook legs and attempt to pull opponent's leg to the floor.

Two Handle Tug-of-War
Pull your opponent across the line. Use individual tug-of-war ropes.

Rat Tail Ball Dribbling
Step on your opponent's rope while dribbling a ball. Make "tail" fall to the ground.

Ball Dribbling Flag Pulling
Pull your opponent's flag while you are both dribbling a ball.

Rooster Fight #1
Opponents hop on one foot, arms folded across chest. Jousting continues until one person puts foot down.

Rooster Fight #2
Opponents hop on one foot, hands behind back, bumping until one person puts both feet down.

Rooster Fight #3
Opponents hop on one foot, pulling and releasing tug-of-war rope. First person to force the other to put both feet down in two rounds wins.

Rooster Fight #4
Opponents hop around attempting to cause other person to put both feet down. Each contest is won with two rounds.

Rooster Fight #5
Opponents joust with pillows while hopping on one foot. Game is over when one person touches down both feet.

Rooster Fight #6
Opponents joust with 8½" balls while hopping on one foot. Game is over when one person touches down both feet.

Quick Spin and Pull Flag
Stand back-to-back, hands on head. On "Go" turn and pull opponent's flag.

Wand Push
Try to push your opponent off a line, rope, or 2"x 4" board.

Cylinder Jousting
Opponents begin on the low board with cylinders on one hand. Continue until one person steps down.

129

Scale

Elbow Dip

Corkscrew

Jump Foot

Knee Walk

Dip

Knee Dip

Jump 'n Slap Heels

Simple Stunts

Single Squat

Egg Sit or V Sit

Bells

Through the stick

Knuckle Down

Jump 'N Reach

Jump and Touch

One Foot Balance

Coffee Grinder

Cut the Wand

Bear Dance

Grasp the Toe

Thread the Needle

Up Spring

Turk Stand

Crane Dive

Back to Back Stand

Roll Over Your Partner

Hold Out

Greeter

1. 2. 3. 4. 5. 6.

Wring the Dishrag

Double Knee Bend Walk

Bent Knee Stand

Cooperative Activities

Human Spring

Table Balance

Chair Sit On Feet and Hands

Horizontal Stand

Two Down the Stick Wheelbarrow

Dromedary

Belly Swan Balance

Centipede

Partner Pull Up

Double Forward Roll

Churn the Butter

Human Ball

131

Two Point Balance

Forward Roll

Backward Roll

Forward Roll Variations

Mat Activities

Backward Roll Variations

Backbend from Prone Position

Limber

Back Bend from Standing Position

Round-Off

Head Balance

Cartwheel

Handspring

Head Balance to Swan

Alligator Walk

Crab Walk

Seal Walk

Frog Hop

Bear Walk

Cat Walk

Animal Walks

Measuring Worm

Turtle Walk

Kangaroo Walk

Lame Kangaroo Walk

Elephant Walk

Lame Dog Walk

Ostrich Walk

Rabbit Hop

Gorilla Walk

Sneaky Snake

Penguin Walk

Panther Walk

Parachute Activities
Locomotor Skills - Arm and Shoulder Strength
Flexibility - Endurance

Hand Grips

1. Over Hand

2. Underhand

3. Alternating

Starting Positions

1. Ostrich Position
   One - two - three -
   lift!

2. Waist Level Position
   One - two - three -
   lift!

Where to grip parachute

Always grip the para-
chute close to the seam.

Ripples and Waves

Small - large

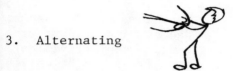

Warm-up activity:
Shake the parachute
"vigorously."

Locomotor Activities
Run, Walk, Jump, Hop,
Skip, Gallop, Slide...

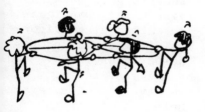

Direct your students
to grasp the parachute
with right - left hand
and move in a circle.
Integrate motor skills
with music. "Aerobic
Activities"

Popcorn

Place different types of
balls on the parachute.
Shake the parachute until
the balls all bounce off
and onto the ground.

Wiffle Balls are great!
Game Activity - Make the
balls bounce off on your
opponent's half of the
parachute.

Cloud

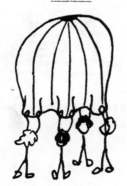

Students begin in ostrich
position. One - two -
three - lift! When the
parachute is inflated
students walk in 3 to 5
steps on command: Walk
1, 2, 3, 4, 5.

Ball Roll

Place a ball on the para-
chute. The class cooper-
atively lifts the parachute
at different intervals
in order to keep the ball
rolling in a circle around
the edge of the parachute.

Sun Flower

Students begin in
ostrich position and
inflate parachute. When
the parachute is inflated
students take 3 steps
forward and quickly bring
the parachute to the
ground and kneel down on
the outside edge. All
players join hands and
lean in and out on command
to represent a sunflower
seed.

Dome

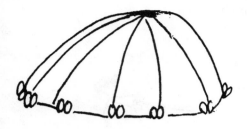

Students begin in
ostrich position and
inflate parachute.
When the parachute
is inflated, students
take 3 steps forward,
turn quickly, change
grips and quickly bring
the parachute to the
ground while they kneel
or sit inside.
"Nobody Home"

Up! Up! and Away

Students begin in
ostrich position and
inflate parachute.
When the parachute is
inflated, students
take one or two steps
forward and release
parachute on command.
The parachute remains
suspended for a few
seconds. Imagination -
The class decides what
animal, monster, or
creature the parachute
resembles after it falls
to the ground.

Dance Steps

Marching, circle dances,
dances without partners,
imagination activities
can all be taught while
students are holding the
parachute waist-high.

Arm Strength and Endurance Activities

Parachute Pull

Students all pull
at the same time
and hold count
for 10 seconds.

Turn Around Pull

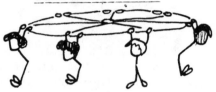

Students grasp parachute
and face outward while
holding parachute over-
head. On signal, all
students pull and hold
count for 10 seconds.

Roll-up

Students hold parachute
waist high. On signal,
the entire class vigor-
ously rolls and unrolls
the parachute. This coul
be the last activity of
the day. Put the para-
chute away after the
last roll.

Sit Ups

Students sit down
with legs placed
underneath the para-
chute while grasping
the parachute with
over hand grip. On
command, all students
perform sit ups.

Circuit and Interval Training

The parachute placed on
the floor is in perfect
position for total class
training. Perform
strength and endurance
activities in place on
cue, jog around perimeter
of parachute. Sit ups,
push ups, jumping jacks,
windmill, side bends are
but a few of the statuing
and astronaut activities
that can be performed.

Total Relaxation

The parachute is placed
flat on the floor.
Students can lie on top
of the seam and the
teacher can present tota
relaxation activities to
close the end of the
physical education perio

Cone and Cord Maze
Crawl under-over.
Tie fishing weights
on the ends of the
cord to keep them
tight.

Scoops
and
Fluff Balls

Hoop or bike tire pattern
with a rope return.

Twister

Hoop Holder

Instant **Gross Motor** Station Ideas

Tin Can Stilts

Foot Launcher

Mat Activities

Balloon Center

Fluff Ball – Waste Baskets
Target Toss

Multi-purpose Room Chair Maze

Walking Board
Challenges

Tennis Ball String Wand

Locomotor Skill Station - Total continuous
circuit created from multi-purpose room equipment.

Low Waters

Beach ball juggling. Knee, foot, head. Cooperative or individual.

Tumbling

Keep it up. Nylon stocking paddles and wadded up ditto paper.

Wall Dodge Station

Rhythm Stick Station

Fluff Ball

No Dribble Basketball
Students make the hoop out of a coat hanger and string net.
Students creat rules.
One-on-on, two-on-two.
Other activities: Free throw, Horse, 21, Eyes Closed, Block a Shot.

Eskimo YoYo Challenge Center

Jacks

Chair Ring Toss

Bolero

Jump the Shot

stack the Chips
Stack the chips on your elbow, snap out your arm. Can you catch them all?

Indoor Frisbee

Foot Twist

Hold pin up to your chin.

Clothes Pin Drop into a tennis ball can.

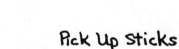

Pick Up Sticks

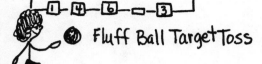 Fluff Ball Target Toss

 Jump Rope Practice

Partner tricks

Leap the Brook

See page—

 Rebounding

 Limbo and long turning rope activities.

Fly back

 Walk the Rope - Pass your partner, challenge activities.

 Tennis ball - Styrofoam Cup Bowling. Styrofoam cups taped together.

Ropes

see page

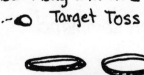 Bean Bag and Tire Target Toss

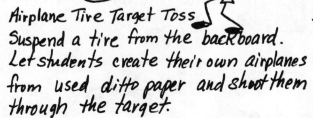 Airplane Tire Target Toss
Suspend a tire from the backboard. Let students create their own airplanes from used ditto paper and shoot them through the target.

 Triangle Football

 Nylon stocking paddle and padded up piece of ditto paper. Create your own game center.

 Pois-Pois Center
See page
Students create their own routine.

Balance Block Center

Balance block - 4×4×4", Styrofoam cups. Students create challenges for each other.

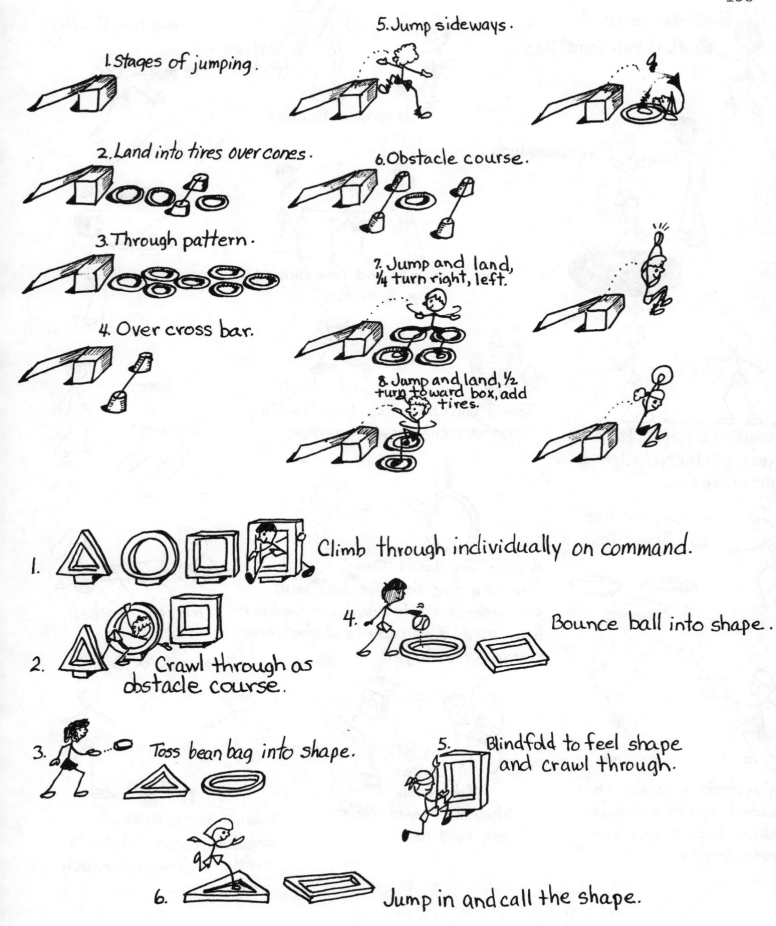

1. Stages of jumping.

2. Land into tires over cones.

3. Through pattern.

4. Over cross bar.

5. Jump sideways.

6. Obstacle course.

7. Jump and land, ¼ turn right, left.

8. Jump and land, ½ turn toward box, add tires.

1. Climb through individually on command.

2. Crawl through as obstacle course.

3. Toss bean bag into shape.

4. Bounce ball into shape.

5. Blindfold to feel shape and crawl through.

6. Jump in and call the shape.

Walk on rungs

Crawl on rungs spaces

Jump between rungs
Hands and feet on rungs

Crawl between rungs

Crab walk on outside of rungs/on rungs.

Travel down ladder using 3 parts of body/4 parts/2 parts

Walk on outside and bounce ball between rungs.

walk up incline box on all fours.

Walk on ladder with bean bag on head.

Tire patterns for bouncing

Toss and Catch

Hoops Vertical

Crawl through shapes

Over   Bean   Under
         Bag

Bounce ball in shapes

Tires

Tracking

Gross Motor and Perceptual Motor Equipment
Set Up and Activities

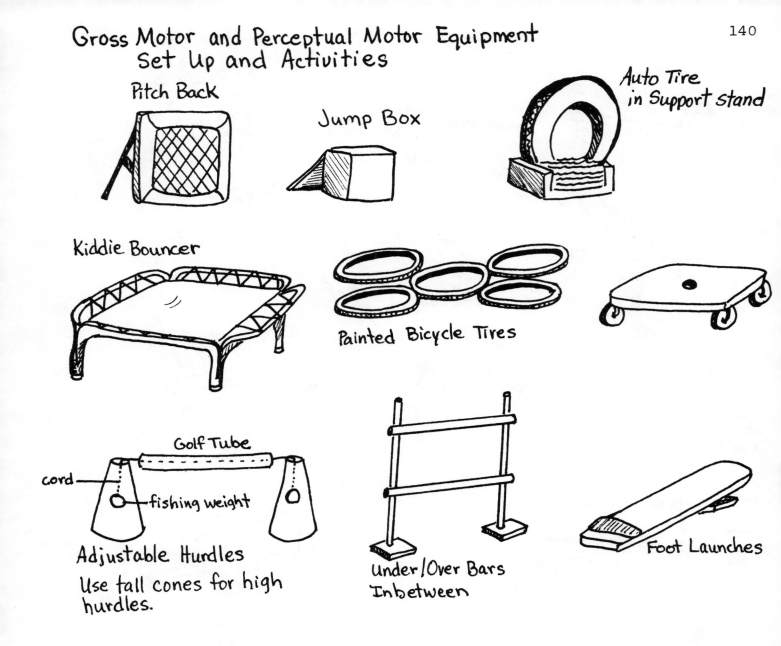

Pitch Back

Jump Box

Auto Tire in Support stand

Kiddie Bouncer

Painted Bicycle Tires

cord — fishing weight
Golf Tube

Adjustable Hurdles
Use tall cones for high hurdles.

Under/Over Bars Inbetween

Foot Launches

For complete Perceptual Motor program see Jack Capon materials, Front Row Experience, Pubs.

Student Profile

Date _____ Locomotor Skills Teacher _____ Student's Name	1. CRAWLING	2. CREEPING	3. WALKING	4. RUNNING	5. HOPPING	6. GALLOPING	7. SKIPPING	8. JUMPING	9. SLIDING	10. LEAPING	COMMENTS

Cooperative stilts

Balance Items

1. Tin Can Stilts

From Tuna Cans → to Coffee Cans

Tin Can Clompers
1,2,3, lb. coffee cans

Choose the level of can for your student's ability. Punch holes in can with a can opener.

Pull cord through holes using the right length for your students:

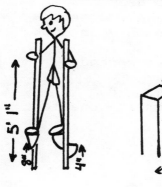

Tin Can Stilt Tag

If a player gets within a foot of another player, the player is considered tagged.

2. Wooden Stilts

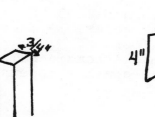

5' 1"

3/4"

3"
4"

Foot Pads

Foot pads are screwed through stilt into foot pad. Use 2" - 2½" screws.

Dramatic Balance. Various Types of cans and levels will provide more variations. Teacher must constantly supply some type of activity through challenge to keep the tin can stilts interesting.
Examples:

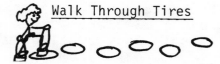

Walk Through Tires

Walk backward through tires

Step Over the Rope

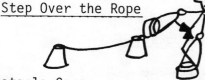

Total Obstacle Cans

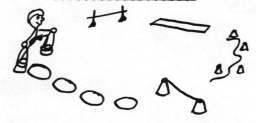

Dramatic Balance. A parent help project. Constant challenge and stimuli must be provided through challenge for students who are ready to go ahead.

Low Walking Board Combative Activities

Pillow Push

Force opponent to step down

Rope Jousting

Force opponent to step down

Cylinder Push

Force opponent to step down

BALANCE ITEMS (Continued)

Wand Push

Force Opponent
to step down

Hand Push or Fake

Push or fake push

Board Bump

Stand sideways
bump opponent off

Balance Boards

Balance boards are 3/4" thick and 16" square
with bottom blocks 4" x 4" with various
heights of 2", 3", and 4". A good Static
Balance item - many small challenges can be
asked.

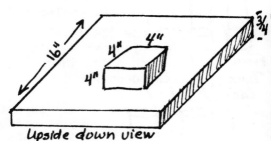

Upside down view

Balance Board Combative Activities

Rope Jousting

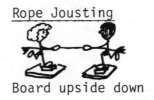

Board upside down

Stump Pull Off

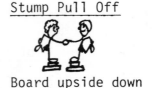

Board upside down

Pillow Push

Board upside down

Balance Board Challenges

1. Balance yourself for 10 seconds
2. Balance yourself for 10 seconds while looking straight ahead
3. Balance and touch your knees, hips, shoulders, and head
4. Balance for 15 seconds on your best foot - now touch your sock
5. Balance for 15 seconds on your other foot - now touch your sock
6. Balance, both feet, bounce and catch a ball 3 times
7. Balance on your toes for 15 seconds, relax, 15 more seconds
8. Balance - move the board ahead one foot
9. Balance - spin the board ½ way around - remain balanced
10. Balance - slide your feet together - apart - together - one foot
    balance . . . .
11. Close your eyes and . . . .

Low Walking Board Challenges

Walk forward down the board. This time, keep your eyes on my hand. Now,
follow my hand with your eyes as you walk down the board. Walk forward to
center of board - turn around. Walk backward to the end. Walk backward
down the board, keeping your eyes on my hand. Walk sideways down the
board - now, sideways with other side forward. Walk forward with your arms
to your side - backward. Take the wand and balance with it as you walk.
Hold the wand on one end and balance with wand sticking out to side. Put
2 deck rings on and walk with the wand to side - now other side - now,
backward. Walk forward and step over the crossbar. Walk backward and
step over the 6" high crossbar or rope. Walk down the beam with the same
foot in front, using the wand and deck rings. Now, try it backward.

Walk forward, pick up the (eraser - bean bag) in the middle of the board and put it on your head. Walk backward, bend down, reach behind you, and pick up the bean bag. Put it on your head and continue. Walk forward and backward with the bean bag on your head.

Hold the rope 3' high and have student walk down the board and under the rope. How low can you go? Walk under rope with hands clasped behind your body - backward. Hop down the board on your best foot - other foot. Walk to the center of the beam - swan balance, high balance, low balance, best foot, other foot, eyes closed. Place a bean bag on your head. Walk over the rope, under the rope, over the rope. Do it backwards. Cat walk down the board on all fours. Fold a piece of paper in half and place it in the center of the board so that it stands up. Walk to center, kneel. Pick it up with your teeth. Rise and walk to the end. Walk slowly down the board with your eyes closed (or blindfolded).

Partners start at opposite ends of board - pass each other without falling off. Get a 7" ball - make up some ball dribbling, board walking, challenges for your friends.

WOODEN STILT CHALLENGES

Can you -

1. Mount the stilts without help
2. Stay up on the stilts for 30 seconds without help
3. Take 15 steps forward
4. Walk around the cones and back
5. Walk through the tires
6. Take 15 steps backward
7. Walk sideways around the cones
8. Walk sideways through the hoops
9. Walk backward around the cones
10. Walk backward through the hoops
11. Step over the 1' high rope, etc.
12. Try balancing on one stilt
13. Make yourself very low - very tall - on stilts
14. Pretend that you are marching on your stilts
15. Walk along a painted line, walk the basketball court, the big circle
16. Walk with stilts close together - stilts wide apart
17. Try hopping on your stilts
18. Change directions every time that I blow the whistle.

Obstacle Course:

Set up an obstacle course - cones, tires, hoops, tennis ball cans, ropes, tetherball poles, etc. Use a stop watch to increase challenge.

Activity #1 Balance Inside a tire

Activity #2 Stilt Races

Activity #3 Obstacle Course

Activity #4 Shuttle Relay

Activity #5 Stilt Tag

Striking Tools

Striking, Tapping, Paddling, etc

1. <u>Nylon Stocking Paddle</u>

Made with a nylon stocking, old coat hanger and tape. Pull the coat hanger into a diamond shape -   Stretch the nylon stocking tightly   over the coat hanger. Tape the nylon   stocking down on the handle. Cut   part of the handle off. Tape over the handle until you have a grip. Some paper wrapped on handle prior to taping may save a lot of tape. Use with a light ball. Keep It Up - Keep It Up with Partners. Primary Paddle - could be indoor used with a balloon.

2. <u>Wooden Tennis Paddle</u>

Use with tennis ball or wiffle ball. Make or purchase. This paddle can be made from 3/8" thick plywood, about 8" in diameter and 10" in length (durable). The handle can be 5-1/2" long and 1" thick.

<u>Paddle Activities</u>

1. <u>Low Net</u>

Paddle Tennis
Try a wiffle ball

2. <u>Ball Wall</u>

Practice or paddle
tennis

3. <u>Paddle Ball or Poor Man's JoKari</u>

staple nail
Fishing swivel

Block

The block can be 3½" wide, 3½" high, and 5½" long

Cost about $ 5.00 to make - total
Cost about $15.00 to purchase

Replacement ball and string bought at Penney's Sporting Goods Department, Jokari Equipment. Put a small fishing swivel on the block to avoid twisting string.

4. <u>Old Tennis Racquets</u>   Use old tennis racquets for:

<u>Tennis Baseball</u>

Teacher pitches-
Make hitter successful

4 or 5 tennis balls
on hand, one strike
or two foul balls

<u>High Flies</u>

Tennis racquets,
scoop and tennis
balls

Teacher hits "High
Flies" to players in
the field. Players
track balls, catch
them in scoops.

<u>Ball Wall</u>
Striking practice

Racquet, tennis balls,
wall

5. <u>Toilet Brushes</u>   This is an inexpensive purchase item.

<u>Toilet Brush Hockey</u>

Can also be played on
scooter board. Wiffle
ball, fluff ball, hockey
puck.

6. <u>Old Ping-Pong Paddles</u>

Collection item. Can be used for paddle
challenge. Can also be used for Ping-
Pong Paddle Hockey with fluff balls.
Four Ball Hockey - players work extremely
hard. Also, relays pushing balls.

7. <u>Old Brooms</u>

Collection item. Cut handles down. Can
be used for Broom Hockey, Broom Relays,
both sweeping the ball and riding the
broom.

8. <u>Plastic Bats</u>

An item that you probably have around the
school. Can be used for Plastic Bat
Hockey with a sportfoam ball and relays.

9. <u>Fly Backs</u>

Inexpensive purchase item at Gemco or K
Mart. Good eye/hand coordination item.

10. <u>Poor Man's P.V.C. Pipe Hockey Sticks</u>

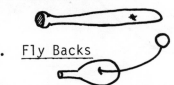

Hockey sticks are easy to make out of pvc
pipe and are more durable than commercial
sticks. Use with homemade pucks.

11. <u>Boomer Bat</u>

A bat that can be used to hit a 4, 5, or
6" red rubber ball, a mile. A <u>5th-6th
grade item</u>.
Use a plastic fresh water bottle and a
softball bat filed down and pushed inside.
A screw is inserted at bottom of bottle
and 3 screws are inserted through neck
of bottle into bat.

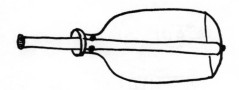

12. __Pepsi Bat__

Could be any "liter" soft drink bottle. A 1 liter plastic bottle and 24" doweling. Shorten the doweling down to your primary class level. Great for T-Ball off of the cones for your 1st graders. Put a screw in bottom and 3 screws through neck into dowels. Easy to replace.

13. __Poor Man's Pillo Polo Sticks__

A liter bottle and 18" dowels. Dowels come 36" long. Cut them in half, force them into bottles. Put a screw in bottom and 3 screws through neck and into dowel. A very easy item to fix when a bottle cracks. Your entire class can play 4 ba Pillo Polo at a low cost - just the price of the dowels. NOTE: Dowels are not always uniform in width. If you have difficulty forcing dowel into neck of bottle heat the neck by putting it into a pan of boiling water for about 1 minute, only. Then force the dowel in.

14. __Fat Bat__

A plastic "Fat Bat" for wiffle ball soft ball. Great success! Can be purchased at Gemco or K Mart. Also great for T-Ba and Topple Ball off of a cone or old bat ting tee.

__T Ball__

Teacher makes up the rules for T Baseball at that level. T-Ball can be played off of a tall cone.

__Topple Ball__

Batter defends object on T or cone from all directions. Knock the ball off and replace the batter.

__Fat Bat Wiffle Ball Softball__

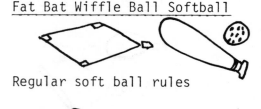

Regular soft ball rules

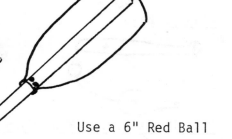

Boomer Bat Baseball!
Three Flies Up!
Over The Line!
"Everybody Hits"

Use a 6" Red Ball

__Floor and Field Pucks__

1. Two Clorox bottles, bottoms taped together.
2. Two old frisbees taped together. Coil some old rope inside to add weight.
3. Erasers, sponges, foam taped together

Other Types of Low Budget, Collected, and Homemade Equipment

General Equipment that will add to Program Efficiency. All of the equipment listed below is considered low budget, around town purchases - collected - homemade.

Indoor Frisbee #1
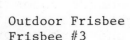

Purchase pre-cut foam from Standard Brands Paint or Handyman type stores. "Instant Indoor Frisbee"

Indoor Frisbee #2

Back Pack or Pocket Frisbee - easily folds, non-threatening. Kids can bring them indoors. Ours were donated by a company that used them for promotional purposes.

Outdoor Frisbee
Frisbee #3

Plastic (regular frisbees) can be purchased inexpensively - promotional item purchased at the auction. Kids can bring them in to class. Ours (100) were donated by a Savings and Loan Company as a promotional item. Create your own activities . . . .

Carpet Squares

Carpet remnant stores always have sales. Teachers can usually talk salespeople into a good deal. Great for instant circles. Spaces for musical squares, swat, and other floor activities. 12" x 12" squares are great for personal space items for primary children.

Classroom
Wastebasket

Classroom wastebaskets for Target Pass Games: <u>Swat</u> and <u>Trash Can Dodgeball</u>.

Swatter

Swatter - rolled up newspaper (flimsy) and taped with masking tape. Instant movement item 30-30 (imaginary wands)

Ball Bags

Ball Bags can be from gunny sacks donated to you by the feed store. Tie a cord through the top of the bag and Presto - Instant Ball Bag. Old laundry bags can also be used.

Blind Folds
12" elastic -
durable cloth

Blind folds are great items to make for various activities - trust Walks around school, blind relays, and obstacle courses. Marco Polo Games, Prui, Memory Activities, Touch-Feely Activities, What is it.

Car Inner Tube
Blindfold - Cut
the band 2" thick
on the front side.

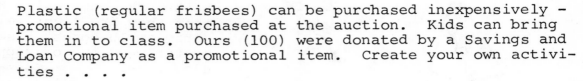

Rattler Cans Games - Match the Sounds, Smell too. Marco Polo Tag in a circle. The player shakes the can; the closest player must respond with noise from his/her can. Blindfolds on.

Rattler Cans -
Tennis ball cans;
Lid or taped top

8. 4-Station Steal the Bacon Junk
    Manipulative Items - Two of
    anything

Paddles   Pillo Polo   Old Brooms

Pucks:
Old   Chalk   Taped   Deck

Sponge   Eraser   Foam   Ring

Steal the bacon items for sweeping,
stroking, scooping items across your own
line. Students are numbered from 1-4
instead of 1-15. Lines turn over - move
players to new stations.

Other General Homemade Equipment that will add to Program Efficiency. All of
the equipment listed below can be made by the teacher or a parent group.

9. Homemade Cones

Homemade cones are a great general piece
of physical education equipment. The
best part about using homemade cones is
that they are light weight. No one mind
carrying 10 cones. Use the dark colored
posterboard out of supply that no one
else uses.

10. Football Flags - Durable Cloth

Flags are great for all chasing, fleeing
games. They help to curb arguments, "I
tagged you." "No you didn't." Hem the
edges for greater durability. The quick
est way to have 2 colors is to dye one
end. If you use 2 colors for flags that
are cut at specified lengths, the short
color goes into the pocket with a little
of the short color showing. Everyone
will have the same length of flag when
they participate.

11. Pinnies - Durable Cloth

Pinnies are used for team identification
One team wears pinnies, the other doesn
Pinnies must be easy to put on and take
off. That is why there are no tie stra
for the waist.

12. Plastic or Metal Containers

Used for storage containers and for
throwing into practice. Health food
stores keep nuts, flour in this type of
container. Or use classroom waste bask

13. Bolero   Double
                    Bolero

Stand on a chair. Around the world.

An eye-hand coordinate tool. A nut can
and old ball that is smaller than the c
and a piece of cord or elastic.

14. Streamers - 5-6 feet of
    surveyor's tape

Great tool for developing cross lateral
movements. Patterning, mirroring, rhythm, concentrating on directions.

½ of a plastic golf club protector
tube

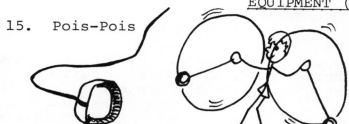

15. Pois-Pois

Another eye-hand coordination tool made from 4" foam pipe insulation. Slice it 1" thick. Use the paper cutter. Tie a 2 - 3" piece of cord to each slice and <u>Zap</u> - you have a set of Pois-Pois. (The foam does not hurt when a player gets hit.)

POIS-POIS CHALLENGE ACTIVITIES

One Pois:

1.   One hand - side - front - other side - other hand
2.   One hand - side - front - other side - switch hands - do not stop
3.   Go around body - waist - knees - switch hands - reverse
4.   Helicopter - reverse - other hand - both hands - continuous
5.   Figure eights - left hand - right hand - both hands - continuous
6.   Jump the shot by yourself
7.   Short helicopters - right in front of you - waist high - other hand
8.   Wind each finger - adding a finger each reverse wind
9.   Land your helicopter - knees - sit down - lie down - one side - get up
10. Helicopter - take off position - rise - take off - gallop - skip slide
11. Helicopter - bounce up and down
12. Throwing tricks - let go and catch - let go under knee and catch
13. Poor Man's Lemon Twist - Toe Twirl

Two Pois:

1.   Side wheelers - forward/backward
2.   Double helicopters - land - one knee - other knee - up
3.   Double Pois - crossies
4.   Double Pois - chasies
5.   Double Pois - jump the shot
6.   Jump the shot and sidewinder
7.   Sidewinder - toss 2 - catch 2

Cooperative Presentations

Children love to get into groups, work up routines to records, and present their routines.

Imagination

How would you look if you had -
      The world's largest eyes
      The world's largest earrings
      A rock singer . . . .

Children will invent popular things

16. Scarves for Beginning Juggling

Scarves are great tools to use for beginning juggling. They provide student with more time to get it together before they fall. A collection item from students, a purchase item from K Mart type stores.

17. Juggling Balls

Sand

filled with sand

Use old tennis balls. Poke a hole in the tennis balls with teacher's scissors. Push a small funnel into the hole. Pour sand into the ball. Tape the hole and zap - you have a juggle ball. Sand-filled tennis balls are easier to juggle and they do not bounce all over the room when they are dropped.

18. Individual Tug of War Ropes

To make individual tug of war ropes, you first need to locate some disposable "garden hose" and "old rope." Cut the garden hose into 18" lengths; cut the rope into 8 - 9' lengths. Push the rope through the hose and tie off ends of rope. See diagram.

18A. Truck Tire Inner Tube Tug of War Rope

2" strips tied together for 2 person tug-of-war. Tie 3 or 4 together for 3 or 4 person tug-of-war.

INDIVIDUAL TUG-OF-WAR ACTIVITIES

1. Bull Dog Pull

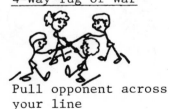

Pick up can

2. Rooster Fight

Make opponent put foot down

3. Off Balance

Make opponent step off board

4. Balance Board

Pull opponent off balance. Balance board is turned upside down.

5. Tug of War

Pull opponent across line

6. Two Rope Horse Pull

Pull opponent across line

7. 4-Way Tug of War

Pull opponent across your line

8. Jump the Shot

Cooperation

9. Rooster Fight

Make opponent put foot down

19. Foot Twists

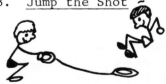

Great coordination item. Would be great have a few in the Ball Box. Cut a 14" piece of tubing. Glue ends together by overlapping opening with a larger piece tubing. Poke a hole in tennis ball with scissors. Cut clothes line wire 20" long Tie a knot in end, force it in the ball. Wrap the other end around circle of tubi Tie end and tape.

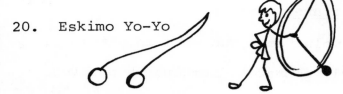

20. Eskimo Yo-Yo

Tennis balls tied on two cords with the cords tied together. Cords 1½' to 2' long. Hold end in one hand, balls go around in circle in opposite directions just missing each other.

21. Bleach Bottle Scoops

The scoop can be made from plastic bottles. They are made by cutting a portion of the plastic bottle off at the bottom, then cutting a slant toward the handle.

Hand/Eye

Scoop 4 - Square with Bean Bags or Tennis Balls

High flies with Tennis Racquet, Tennis Balls and Scoops

Players

Way out on grass

Teacher stands on edge of blacktop

Tossing and Catching

Scoop Basketball Bombardment

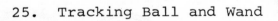

(Use trash cans from behind cafeteria.) Place the bottom of first can upside down, put the second can on top. Use ropes or chalk off circle for goal tending area. No reaching over barrels to catch ball with scoop. To make upward tosses and scoop balls into opponents goal. No Goal Tending!

22. Poor Man's Trac Ball or LaCrosse Stick

Take scoop to hardware store for measurement of opening & pvc pipe.

A durable swimming pool chemical bottle similar to a Clorox bottle and a 2' piece of lightweight pvc pipe that fits into the opening. Glue it, nail it, tape it into the opening. Presto - a Trac Ball Racquet or LaCrosse Stick. Use tennis balls.

23. Clorox Bottle Rumble Rhumbas

Another use for the scoops. Scoops tie to your waist, use with a tennis ball. 30-30 challenge or center activity. See Rumble Rhumba Activities.

24. Paper Rollers

Balance item, roll on two, balance combatives.

25. Tracking Ball and Wand

26. Perceptual Motor - Under/Over Bars or Limbo Standards

Any wand and a suspended ball. Use tracking ball with low walking board also.

27. Adjustable Hurdles

For perceptual motor program. Pvc pipe or golf tube hurdle, cord and weights.

28. Foot Launchers

Great eye/foot item.

29. Physical Fitness Exerciser

Made by Carl Phelps, Sacramento City School District.

30. Task Card Holder

9 x 12" masonite board with a ledge to hold task cards in upright position.

EQUIPMENT (Continued)

31. Direction Cards — For volunteers who work in stations.

32. Floor Matrix — Vinyl, alphabet, numbers, hopscotch.

33. Chinese Jump Ropes — Make from streth cord purchased at State Surplus.

34. Lids — Orange juice cans for lagging activities.

35. Scooter Boards — Multiple uses, perceptual motor programs, relays, basketball, hockey, etc.

36. Movement Education Cards — Directionality, Bones, Designs in Space, Muscles, body parts, locomotor, manipulative movements, toss n catch, Record Imagination Cards - Rocky.

37. Hi Fli Nets — Pvc pipe frame with 15" x 15" canvas as n Inside rubber bands and S hooks. Works great with a tennis ball, other balls wil rebound slower.

38. Ball Bags — Old gunny sacks or laundry sacks. Tie a cord through top for an instant ball bag.

39. Poor Man's Jousting Tool - Bataca — Foam rubber roll. Put one hand in each e or use just one end.

40. Yarn Spool Cones — Can be targets for tossing or tennis ball bowling or for objects to pick up off the balance blocks.

Traditional Standard Purchase Equipment - Central Storage

Ball Pump
Purchase Item

Ball Bags

Line Marker
Should belong
to several schools

Stop Watch
One per school

School Price $19.74

Whistle

Measuring Tape

Wiffle Ball (boxed)

Football (bagged)

Basketball (bagged)

Volleyball (bagged)

Soccer ball (bagged)

Parachute (boxed)

7" Red Ball (bagged)

8" Red Ball (bagged)

Volleyball nets (boxed)

Cones (stacked)

Kickball (bagged)

Sport-foam Ball
(bagged)

Softball (boxed)

Bats (boxed)

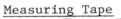

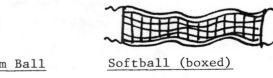
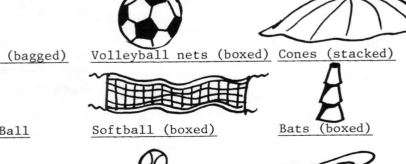

Sample Report Cards

KINDERGARTEN PHYSICAL EDUCATION PROGRESS REPORT	FIRST GRADE PHYSICAL EDUCATION PROGRESS REPORT

KINDERGARTEN PHYSICAL EDUCATION PROGRESS REPORT

STUDENT NAME _____ ROOM NO. _____

SCHOOL _____ TEACHER _____

SYMBOLS:

- O – Outstanding   Yes – Can execute
- S – Satisfactory   No – Cannot execute
- N – Needs to improve

Locomotor Skills
- Walk
- Run
- Jump
- Hop
- Skip
- Gallop
- Leap
- Slide

Stunts – Tumbling
- Spatial relationships
- Balance
- Body awareness

Manipulative
- Catching
- Throwing
- Striking
- Bouncing
- Jump rope – long
- Jump rope – short

Rhythms
- Interpret and respond to beat, tempo and pitch of music

Game Skills
- Knows information – tag and dodge

Multidisciplinary
- Identifies and names 10 skeletal parts

Social Skills
- Ability to lead and follow
- Willingly participates
- Consideration of self, others and equipment
- Ability to listen and follow directions

FIRST GRADE PHYSICAL EDUCATION PROGRESS REPORT

STUDENT NAME _____ ROOM NO. _____

SCHOOL _____ TEACHER _____

SYMBOLS:

- O – Outstanding   Yes – Can execute
- S – Satisfactory   No – Cannot execute
- N – Needs to improve

Locomotor Skills
- Walk
- Run
- Jump
- Hop
- Skip
- Gallop
- Leap
- Slide

Stunts – Tumbling
- Fall safely
- Climb 10 feet on climbing rope
- Individual tumbling activities
- Balance

Manipulative
- Catching
- Throwing – overhand
- Striking
- Ball bouncing
- Jump rope – long
- Jump rope – short

Rhythms – Locomotor and Non-Locomotor
- Response and interpretation to beat, temp and pitch of muisc

Game Skills
- Tag – Dodge stop and change directions with control
- Create a game

Multidisciplinary
- Identifies and names skeletal parts

Social Skills
- Ability to lead and follow
- Willingly participates
- Consideration of self, others and equipment
- Listen and follow directions
- Sportsmanship

Sample Report Cards

SECOND/THIRD GRADE PHYSICAL EDUCATION PROGRESS REPORT

STUDENT NAME _____ ROOM NO. _____

SCHOOL _____ TEACHER _____

SYMBOLS:

O - Outstanding   Yes - Can execute
S - Satisfactory   No - Cannot execute
N - Needs to improve

Locomotor Skills
Combines skills of hopping, skipping and galloping, continuously forward and backward

Stunts - Tumbling
Climb 15 feet on climbing rope
Executes tumbling stunts showing flexibility, coordination, strength and agility on indoor and outdoor apparatus

Manipulative
Catching
Throw overhand
Kicking
Striking
Ball handling - simple and complex
Rope jumping - simple and complex

Rhythms
Interpret and respond to beat, tempo and pitch of music
Basic folk and square dance steps

Game Skills
Combines tagging, dodging, stopping and changing directions while using equipment

Strength
Executes 2 or more pull ups (2nd grade)
Executes 3 or more pull ups (3rd grade)
Executes 25 or more bent knee sit ups in one minute
Long jump body length

Social Skills
Ability to lead and follow
Willingly participates
Consideration of self, others and equipment
Listen and follow directions
Sportsmanship

PHYSICAL EDUCATION PROGRESS REPORT GRADES 4, 5, 6

STUDENT _____

TEACHER _____ GRADE _____

SCHOOL _____

SYMBOLS:

O - Outstanding
S - Satisfactory
U - Unsatisfactory

	1st semester	
	1st	2nd
Locomotor Skills		
Body Mechanics		
Stunts - Tumbling		
Physical Fitness		
Game Skills -		
1.		
2.		
3.		
Sport Skills -		
1.		
2.		
3.		
4.		
Responsibility		

	1st	2nd
Development of Skills		
Participation		
Citizenship		